DEMOCRACY AND POWER

Democracy and Power
The Delhi Lectures

Noam Chomsky

OpenBook
Publishers

http://www.openbookpublishers.com

Digital material and resources associated with this volume are available at http://www.openbookpublishers.com/isbn/9781783740925#resources

ISBN Paperback: 978-1-78374-092-5
ISBN Hardback: 978-1-78374-093-2
ISBN Digital (PDF): 978-1-78374-094-9
ISBN Digital ebook (epub): 978-1-78374-095-6
ISBN Digital ebook (mobi): 978-1-78374-096-3
DOI: 10.11647/OBP.0050

Cover image: *The other side of the window* by Varun Chatterji. Wikimedia Commons: http://commons.wikimedia.org/wiki/File:Bandung.jpg

All paper used by Open Book Publishers is SFI (Sustainable Forestry Initiative), and PEFC (Programme for the Endorsement of Forest Certification Schemes) Certified.

Printed in the United Kingdom and United States by Lightning Source for Open Book Publishers (Cambridge, UK).

Contents

Introduction: Chomsky in India

Jean Drèze

Sometime around 1991 I wrote to Noam Chomsky and invited him to give some lectures in India. It felt like wishful thinking – for one thing, I had no idea how his visit would be financed, if he agreed. I did not even expect him to reply, flooded as he must have been with more important mail. So I was pleasantly surprised to receive a short letter from him just a few days later (these were the good old times when real letters were delivered at home by a live postperson). He wrote that he would be happy to come, and that the first week he was free was January 1996 – several years down the line. I wrote back that January 1996 would be fine, and that's when he came.

Easy Guest

Astonishing as it may seem today, Chomsky was not particularly well known in India at that time. Even among left intellectuals, few had paid serious attention to his writings. That was, in fact, one of the reasons why I was hoping that he would accept my invitation. I felt that his ideas needed to be better known in India, where the tenets of Marxism did not do justice to the country's rich experience of popular struggles. There is certainly much to learn from Marx, but it requires some serious suspension of common sense to think that the key to India's social problems today lie in the writings of a nineteenth-century German philosopher. India, of course, has its own galaxy of inspiring thinkers, within as well as outside the Marxist tradition. Yet Chomsky's ideas seemed to me to fill some important gaps. Beyond that, I was hoping that Noam's visit to India would lead to a better appreciation of anarchist thought, which tends to be widely misunderstood.

http://dx.doi.org/10.11647/OBP.0050.07

These hopes have been fulfilled to some extent – Chomsky and other anarchist thinkers are much better known in India today than they were twenty years ago, and I think that his visits have contributed to this. Some leading left intellectuals in India, notably Arundhati Roy (herself strongly influenced by Chomsky), even seem to have anarchist leanings. But there has been some resistance too: in 2001, when Noam visited India again, the venue of one of his lectures had to be shifted from Jawaharlal Nehru University (JNU) to Delhi University at the last minute due to firm opposition from a few faculty members at JNU who seemed to think of him as some sort of "left deviationist."

Others had doubts of a different sort. In October 1997, my friend Milan Rai (who wrote an excellent book on *Chomsky's Politics*) gave a seminar on Chomsky's life and thought at the Centre for the Study of Developing Societies in Delhi. He talked, among other things, about Chomsky's propaganda model and the subversion of democracy. Ashis Nandy commented, "All this is fine, but why do we in India need Noam Chomsky?" I am not sure whether he meant that Chomsky's arguments did not apply in India, or that relying on them would reflect a colonized intellectual mindset. I felt that his question contained its own answer.

For the bulk of his Indian audience, however, Noam Chomsky was mainly a famous scholar they had vaguely heard of. It did not take long for him to win the interest and affection of the Indian public. Soon after his arrival in India on 11 January 1996, his interviews received wide publicity and his lectures attracted larger and larger crowds. After a few days in Delhi he went to Kolkata in West Bengal, where the ruling Communist Party of India (Marxist) made up for the reluctance of some of their comrades at JNU by receiving Noam as a state guest. From there his lecture tour took him to Hyderabad, Chennai, and Thiruvananthapuram, in that order. This book, however, covers the Delhi lectures only.

Noam was a very easy and accommodating guest. He was never worried about where we would put him up, what he would eat or what class he would be travelling. His main concern seemed to be to make good use of his time. When I sent him a draft schedule for his visit, he replied, "One lecture a day is not a full day for me." So we packed more lectures and other engagements in his programme. On 17 January 1996, he gave three lectures in Hyderabad: one on "Intellectuals in the Emerging World Order" at 9.30 am, one on "Globalization and Media" at 3.15 pm and one on "American Foreign Policy" at 7 pm. When I apologized for the low (virtually nil) sight-seeing content of his India programme, Noam wrote back: "No problem... I'll save that for some time when it's more relaxed." I guess that time is yet to come, if it ever does.

I hasten to clarify that Noam did not come to India as a kind of preacher, and certainly not as a preacher of anarchism (none of his lectures were on that subject). He came to share his ideas as well as to learn. The discussion sessions that followed his lectures were always lively and often lasted well beyond the anticipated time (ample extracts are included in this book). In between these engagements, Noam had occasions to learn in other ways. For instance, in West Bengal he spent some time with a rural Gram Panchayat (village council), an experience he greatly appreciated. Alas, much of this happened outside Delhi and is not reflected in this book.

Time Frame

The text printed in this book is very close to the original transcripts of Noam Chomsky's Delhi lectures. Quite a few years have passed since the lectures were delivered. Aside from serial dilly-dallying on my part, publication was delayed because Noam was keen to update these lectures but never got round to it due to innumerable pressing demands on his time (he did correct the original transcripts).

Despite the passage of time, these lectures have not lost their relevance. Along with the question-answer sessions that followed, and the interview reprinted at the end of this book, they cover a vast canvas and provide lasting insights into many aspects of democracy and power in the contemporary world. They can also be seen as an enlightening retrospective on the big events of the twentieth century. Beyond this, the book provides a useful introduction to Chomsky's essential ideas. By the end of it, one feels like a person who had a cataract operation and sees the world in a new light.

In some respects, the interest of these lectures has grown – not diminished – with the passage of time. For instance, they shed useful light on the events that followed the end of the Cold War – events that cast a long shadow on what is happening in the world today. At a time when it was the norm among intellectuals to expect a huge "peace dividend" from the end of the Cold War, Noam Chomsky recognised the situation for what it was, with characteristic clarity: "the disappearance of the Soviet deterrent opened new opportunities for decisive and rapid destruction of much weaker enemies [by the United

States]." This comment goes back to the early 1990s, but it was developed in the Delhi lectures and has applied ever since.

There are many other interesting examples of prescient thoughts in these lectures. Few people in 1996 had a clear sense of the perils of unregulated financial markets – we know something about that today, from bitter experience. Chomsky not only saw the danger but also understood the politics of reckless deregulation better than most economists did at that time (including those who later wrote to the Queen of England, when a financial crisis took them by surprise in 2008, that this was "a failure of the collective imagination of many bright people"). Similarly, there are far-sighted lines in these lectures about the dangers of global warming and environmental destruction. Long before climate change became a household term, Chomsky raised forceful questions about humanity's ability to survive much longer if things continue the way they are. "The prevailing value system," he said eighteen years ago, "is that hegemony is more important than survival." This is all the more true today.

Democracy and Power

It would be presumptuous on my part to attempt a summary of the central ideas of this book. The lectures are packed with insightful thoughts, and what stands out as the central ideas is likely to differ from reader to reader. All I can do is mention a few ideas that seem to be well worth registering.

The lectures are grounded in Noam Chomsky's principled opposition to the concentration of power – whether it is state power, or corporate power, or for that matter the power of the upper castes in Indian society, of men over women in the family, of an unaccountable party leader, or of the boss in the workplace. This is an old anarchist commitment, but Chomsky's formulation of it is particularly appealing: "... any structure of hierarchy and authority carries a heavy burden of justification, whether it involves personal relations or a larger social order. If it cannot bear that burden – sometimes it can – then it is illegitimate and should be dismantled." This sounds to me like a practical and far-reaching principle of thought and action.

Another overarching theme of the lectures, related to the first, is that the concentration of power and privilege is a major threat to democracy.

This, again, is not a new idea, but Chomsky has taken it further than most and applied it with great clarity in numerous contexts. In India, the conflict between democracy and the concentration of power was a major concern of Dr. Ambedkar, who always emphasized that political democracy would be incomplete without economic and social democracy. "Social and economic democracy," he wrote, "are the tissues and the fibre of a political democracy. The tougher the tissue and the fibre, the greater the strength of the body."[1] In this respect, Chomsky and Ambedkar are on the same wavelength, even if their respective ideas also diverge in important ways (for instance, on the role of the state in bringing about economic democracy). It is possibly of interest that both Chomsky and Ambedkar were strongly influenced by John Dewey, who was also deeply concerned with the conflict between democracy and the concentration of power.

A third theme is the specific threat posed by the growth of corporate power and the "new despotism of state-supported private power." Chomsky is uncompromising in his view of private corporations as "unaccountable private tyrannies." Corporate capitalism, as he sees it, is the last survivor of three systems of tyranny that have common roots. The point is well summed up in his concluding comment at the end of the last question-answer session in the book:

> In the twentieth century, three forms of totalitarianism developed: Bolshevism, fascism, and corporations. They really are three forms of totalitarianism. And in fact they have... much the same intellectual roots. They come out of neo-Hegelian ideas about the rights of organic entities over individuals – a big attack on classical liberalism. Well, two of those forms of totalitarianism were overthrown. The third one is rampant. But it's no more engraved in stone than the other two. In fact, I think it's weaker. It doesn't have the same kind of coercive force behind it. So it can be overthrown, too, in favour of democratic control.

How "democratic control" is to be exercised is not something for which Chomsky has a formula or blueprint. Rather, democratic control is a general principle that we can have some hope of applying in gradually widening spheres of social life. This includes replacing authoritarian modes of economic organization with alternative institutions based, for instance, on worker management, voluntary cooperation, participatory planning and the federation principle.

---

1 Ambedkar, B.R. (1946), *What Congress and Gandhi have done to the Untouchables* (Bombay: Thacker & Co), p. 207.

A fourth essential idea is the role of propaganda in enabling private corporations and other centres of power to undermine democracy and maintain their dominance. In his exposition of the basic idea early on in the book, Chomsky quotes the Australian scholar Alex Carey, who inspired his own work on corporate propaganda: "The twentieth century has been characterized by three developments of great political importance: the growth of democracy; the growth of corporate power; and the growth of corporate propaganda as a means of protecting corporate power against democracy."[2] The idea that propaganda is a pervasive tool of control in democratic societies may sound far-fetched to those who are not familiar with Chomsky's writings, because it sounds like a conspiracy theory. But corporate propaganda is not an organised conspiracy. It works mainly through a sort of filtering process whereby those who say the right things (the sort of things corporate bosses like to hear) are able to climb the ladder and the rest are left behind.[3] As a result, a corporate-sponsored mass-media system that superficially looks pluralistic and adversarial actually restricts public debate to a narrow framework that suits the privileged and powerful. As Chomsky points out, the propaganda system includes not only the mass media but also related sectors such as the entertainment industry, and even "extends to a good deal more of scholarship than its practitioners like to admit": scholarly ideas that suit the privileged and powerful (such as the odd notion, common in economics, that rationality and self-interest are more or less synonymous) tend to flourish while ideas that threaten their interests get sidelined. The process is obvious enough, but we are so used to the illusion of a propaganda-free society that it takes some reflection to liberate ourselves from it.

These ideas were developed largely with reference to the United States, the country Noam Chomsky knows best and often focuses on in these lectures. But they are highly relevant to India, too, increasingly so

---

2 Carey, Alex (1997), *Taking the Risk out of Democracy: Corporate Propaganda versus Freedom and Liberty* (Urbana-Champaign: University of Illinois Press), p. 18.
3 The point was nicely made, in a different context, by C. Wright Mills: "The fit survive, and fitness means... conformity with the criteria of those who have already succeeded. To be compatible with the top men is to act like them, to look like them, to think like them: to be of and for them – or at least to display oneself to them in such a way as to create that impression. This, in fact, is what is meant by 'creating' – a well-chosen word – 'a good impression.' This is what is meant – and nothing else – by being a 'sound man,' as sound as a dollar." See Mills, C. Wright (1956), *The Power Elite* (New York: Oxford University Press), p. 141.

as time goes by. Indeed, India is becoming more and more like the United States (the Indian elite's odd model of what a "developed" society looks like). It is certainly in danger of becoming a "business-driven society," as Chomsky aptly describes the United States. And while India is still a vibrant democracy in some respects, the growth of corporate power adds to the fundamental contradictions discussed by Dr. Ambedkar sixty-five years ago. While Chomsky is careful, in these lectures, not to proffer expert advice on India, his ideas are of great help in understanding what is going on in this country.

Just to illustrate, I have found Chomsky's ideas quite helpful in decoding the literature on social programs in the Indian business media. The general refrain (a virtual "party line") is that social programs are a waste of public money – they should be phased out or privatized. This line is followed with remarkable consistency by a long list of seemingly independent columnists who write under the garb of learned and impartial commentators. The real, unspoken script is this: social programs are against business interests, because higher social spending means higher taxes, or higher interest rates, or less public money for corporate handouts ("incentives" as they are called). Business columnists who want to do well (get invitations to corporate-sponsored seminars or TV shows, for instance) have a pretty good idea of what they have to write. Many of their articles have little intellectual merit, whether in terms of arguments or evidence, yet they get a wide hearing because they serve privileged interests. Some are relatively cogent and well-informed, and their authors may believe in good faith that social programs are a waste of money. But even they tend to do well because they say the right things and abstain from advocating (say) higher taxes or minimum wages. It is hard to believe that their interests do not color their views. The outcome is a relentless propaganda war that makes it virtually impossible to have a rational public debate on social programs.

This brief preview would be incomplete without mentioning that the book is not just about the subversion of democracy by unaccountable powers. It is also about how this subversion can be resisted through popular struggles. Chomsky's forthright indictment of concentrated power always goes hand in hand with a basic confidence in the ability of ordinary people to change the world. Indeed, their struggles have already made the world a better place in many ways. Looking to the future, there are vast possibilities for further progress toward "democratic control by ordinary people of every institution, whether it is industry, colleges, commerce, etc." – provided that humanity survives, which is far from guaranteed.

Anarchist Thought and India

Before concluding, let me return briefly to the relevance of anarchism – or rather anarchist thought – to Indian politics and social movements. In India as elsewhere, anarchist thought is widely misunderstood. As Bhagat Singh, one of the few Indian revolutionaries who had explicit anarchist leanings, put it: "The people are scared of the word anarchism. The word anarchism has been abused so much that even in India revolutionaries have been called anarchist to make them unpopular."

How and why the anarchist tradition came to be comprehensively sidelined in India is not entirely clear. The fact is that very few left leaders, writers or activists in India think of themselves as anarchists. And yet it seems to me that many of them have drawn inspiration from anarchist thought in one way or another, and that we would greatly benefit from a more explicit recognition of this anarchist influence – actual and potential.

There are varieties of anarchist thought (some are pretty weird), just as there are varieties of socialist thought; my concern here is with what one might call cooperative anarchism or libertarian socialism. This is more or less the opposite of what anarchism is often claimed to mean by those whose aim, as Bhagat Singh put it, is to make revolutionaries unpopular. This aim is typically achieved by portraying anarchists as impulsive bomb-throwers who want to destroy the state through violent means.[4] Resistance to state authority and oppression is certainly one of the core principles of anarchism. It is also true that many anarchists believe in the possibility of a stateless society, and perhaps even in the need for a violent overthrow of the state. But anarchist thought certainly does not start from there. In fact, as Chomsky has argued, it is even possible for a committed anarchist to lend temporary support to some state institutions vis-à-vis other centres of power: "In today's world, I think, the goals of a committed anarchist should be to defend some state institutions from the attack against them, while trying at the same time to pry them open to more meaningful public participation – and ultimately, to dismantle them in a much more free society, if the appropriate circumstances can be achieved."[5]

---

4   Bhagat Singh did throw a bomb once (in the chamber of the Central Legislative Assembly), but it was little more than a firecracker and the gesture was largely symbolic. There were no casualties.

5   Chomsky (1996), *Powers and Prospects: Reflections on Human Nature and the Social Order* (London: Pluto), p. 75. This statement must be read in light of the

If anarchist thought does not begin with the idea of a stateless society, let alone the violent overthrow of the state, where does it start from? It starts, I believe, from the same point as these lectures – a deep suspicion of all authority and a principled opposition to the concentration of power, whether it is the power of the state, the corporation, the church, the landlord or the head of a family. As Chomsky argues, this does not mean that all authority and power is illegitimate, but it does mean that if it cannot be justified, it must be dismantled.

Some people believe, against all evidence, that power becomes harmless if it is exercised on behalf of the working class. This is the basis of the hope that a "dictatorship of the proletariat" would pave the way for the withering away of the state and a stateless society. The dangers of this idea were exposed early on by anarchist thinkers such as Bakunin, a contemporary of Karl Marx, who said: "I wonder how he [Marx] fails to see... that the establishment of such a dictatorship would be enough of itself to kill the revolution, to paralyze and distort all popular movements."[6]

The fact that anarchist thinkers predicted with great clarity what would happen in societies based on an apparent dictatorship of the proletariat is not the least reason why it is worth paying more attention to them. Similarly, anarchist thought can help us develop a healthy suspicion of various forms of vanguardism, including the notion that left intellectuals are the vanguard of the proletariat. This notion is of course a terrific deal for intellectuals, since it puts them in command. Vanguardism found fertile soil in India with its long traditions of Brahminism, guru worship, and deference to authority in general. It is, however, at variance with the spirit of anarchism, which includes a basic faith in people's ability to take charge of their own lives and struggles.

Indeed, anarchist thought and libertarian socialism are not limited to a fundamental critique of power and authority – far from it. They also build on constructive ideas about social relations and economic organization, including voluntary association, mutual aid, self-management, and the principle of federation. The basic idea is that a good society would consist,

---

distinction Chomsky makes between "goals" and "visions" (p. 70): "By visions, I mean the conception of a future society that animates what we actually do, a society in which a decent human being might want to live. By goals, I mean the choices and tasks that are within reach, that we will pursue one way or another guided by a vision that may be distant and hazy."

6 Michael Bakunin, letter to *La Liberté*, 5 October 1872; reprinted in Dolgoff, S. (ed.) (1971), *Bakunin on Anarchy* (New York: Vintage Books).

as John Dewey put it, of "… free human beings associated with one another on terms of equality."

One of the most eloquent exponents of the power of free association and voluntary cooperation was Kropotkin, the nineteenth-century anarchist and author of *Mutual Aid*. A zoologist and geographer by profession, Kropotkin spent many years in Siberia, where he noted countless examples of mutual aid among animals. Just to give one example, he observed how, right before the winter, large numbers of deer would gather from hundreds of miles around and congregate at the precise point of a river (the Amur) where it was narrow enough for a large herd to cross safely and reach greener pastures on the other side.[7] He concluded that cooperative behaviour is a plausible outcome of biological evolution – an idea that is being rediscovered today by evolutionary biologists and game theorists.

Kropotkin went on to study cooperation in human societies (which involves much more than biological evolution) and documented in great detail how mutual aid played a pervasive role at all stages of human history, despite being often repressed by the privileged and powerful. More than a hundred years after the publication of *Mutual Aid*, we have many more examples of human activities and institutions based on principles of voluntary association and mutual aid. Anarchist principles of political action have played an important role in the international peace movement, the environmental movement, the fall of the Berlin Wall, the Arab Spring, the Chiapas uprising, the World Social Forum and the right to information movement in India. There have been vibrant experiments with workers' cooperatives and self-management in Spain, Argentina, and Kerala, and there are other examples of economic applications of anarchist principles such as the free software movement. In India, the social organization of many tribal communities is still based on a strong tradition of mutual aid and participatory democracy, evident for instance in institutions like exchange labor and Gram Sabhas.

Even the edifice of electoral democracy rests on a simple act of mutual aid, namely participation in elections: voting does not involve any personal gain for anyone, since a single person's vote cannot influence the outcome of elections, and yet most people do vote, often losing a day's wages and braving long lines, harsh weather or even physical danger. Without mutual cooperation, there would be no democracy, not even the most elementary

---

7   Kropotkin, Peter (1902), *Mutual Aid: A Factor of Evolution* (London: Heinemann), Chapter 2.

form of electoral democracy. As this example illustrates, mutual cooperation does not necessarily require altruism or self-sacrifice; it can also build on simple habits of thought (specifically, habits of sociability and public-spiritedness) that an enlightened society should be able to foster.

Coming back to the left tradition in India, elements of anarchist thought can be found in one form or another in the life and writings of many Indian thinkers, even if they never thought of themselves as anarchists, and indeed were not anarchists. I have already mentioned Bhagat Singh, who had clear anarchist sympathies. To give just a few more examples, Ambedkar was not an anarchist by any means and yet we can find traces of anarchist thought in his writings, for instance his notion of democracy as a "mode of associated living" based on "liberty, equality and fraternity." I think that many anarchists would also be proud of Periyar, who taught people to resist the oppression of caste, patriarchy and religion and to have faith in themselves. Even some leading Marxist thinkers belong here: for instance, Ashok Rudra's critique of "the intelligentsia as a ruling class" has some affinity with Chomsky's analysis of the role of intellectuals in the modern world.

Also within the Marxist tradition, here is something K. Balagopal (one of India's most committed and thoughtful left activists) wrote around the end of his lifelong engagement with a variety of popular struggles:

> What seems to be required are 'localised' (both spatially and socially) movements that are specific enough to bring out the full potential and engender the full self-realisation of various oppressed groups, subsequently federated into a wider movement that can (in a free and democratic way) channelise the aroused energies into a broad movement. This is quite different from the Leninist notion of a single vanguard party that would centralise all knowledge within itself and direct (top down) the struggles of the suppressed masses. In such an effort, the suppressed masses would not even be half awakened to their potential. Even if such a party were to claim that it learns from the people, and even if [it] were to honestly try to do so, the very strategy would be inadequate. If there can at all be a single 'party' which would lead a movement for social transformation, it can only be a federally structured organisation, whose free and equal units would be the political units, centred on the self-directed struggles of various sections of the deprived.[8]

This sounds to me like anarchist thought *par excellence.* As I have illustrated, anarchist principles are alive not just in Indian political thought but also in

---

8 Balagopal, K. (2011), "Popular Struggles: Some Questions for Communist Theory and Practice," in *Ear to the Ground* (New Delhi: Navayana), p. 375.

social life and popular movements. None of this is to say that the time has come to embrace anarchism (or libertarian socialism) and give up other schools of thought. But greater openness to anarchist ideas would certainly bring some fresh air. For instance, I believe that anarchist thought could help us to think more clearly about the relation between caste and class, beware of all authoritarianism, enlarge our understanding of democracy, and open our eyes to the workings of power (for instance, patriarchy and caste discrimination) within our own movements. Last but not least, anarchist thought can inspire us to change the world without waiting for state power, and give us confidence that democratic struggles here and now can be, as Bakunin put it, "the living seeds of the new society which is to replace the old world."

Acknowledgements

These lectures would not have seen the light of day without the help of a few people who generously gave their time to transcribe the recordings, suggest editorial corrections and read successive proofs. Special thanks are due to Reetika Khera, Swati Narayan and Jessica Pudussery. I also take this opportunity to thank all those (too numerous to list) who facilitated Noam Chomsky's visits to India in 1996 and 2001. Different parts of his 1996 lecture tour were kindly sponsored by the Centre for Development Economics at the Delhi School of Economics, the Centre for Applied Linguistics and Translation Studies (University of Hyderabad), the Indian Institute of Technology (Madras), the Centre for Development Studies (Thiruvananthapuram) and *Frontline* magazine. Finally, I am grateful to Anthony Arnove and Alessandra Tosi for facilitating the publication of these lectures by Open Book. It was a pleasure to cooperate with this new publishing venture, which fits well with the spirit of Noam's writings.

An agreeable feature of publishing with Open Book is that it makes it easy to produce new editions with updated material from time to time. We are eagerly hoping that Noam Chomsky will visit India again in early 2015, and if so, an updated edition will be prepared. And who knows, perhaps Noam will get a chance to do some sight-seeing this time!

Jean Drèze
Ranchi, India, October 2014

1. World Orders, Old and New*

What I want to do today is to focus attention on the current scene, but also on its origins, which I think are important for understanding it. So, I want to talk about the world order that arose from the ashes of the Second World War, which is when the current system was established, pretty much in its present form. Perhaps it would be more accurate to say that the world order that was constructed from the ruins of that catastrophe was to an unusual extent (maybe to a unique extent) the product of quite careful and sophisticated planning on the part of business and political leaders, mostly American for obvious reasons. Their planning was quite realistic at that time, as well as being sophisticated and quite successful.

From the turn of the century, the US had been the leading industrial power in the world. It also had enormous resources. During the Second World War, industrial production in the US more than tripled; meanwhile its major competitors were either severely weakened or virtually destroyed. The US had the world's most powerful military force, and had a position of strength and security that probably had no historical parallel. It had firm control of the western hemisphere, it controlled both oceans and beyond the oceans.

The US also largely took control of the Middle East. That was a matter of great significance and remains so to this day. The reason is that, as was understood at that time by the State Department and President Eisenhower, the region is "a stupendous source of strategic power, and one of the greatest material prizes in world history," as well as "probably the richest economic prize in the world in the field of foreign investment." And the US was going to take it over; nobody else was going to interfere there. So the US immediately displaced its traditional rulers. France was simply

---

* Lecture delivered at Jawaharlal Nehru University (New Delhi) on 13 January 1996.

http://dx.doi.org/10.11647/OBP.0050.01

expelled. Britain, for its part, was assigned a certain role which gradually declined as a sort of natural consequence of changes in power relations. Britain became a "junior partner," as the British Foreign Office recognized in an internal document, although illusions about a "special relationship" still persist. The term, not taken very seriously on one side of the Atlantic, was taken quite seriously on the other. On my side of the Atlantic, if you look at the secret documents, Britain is described by a senior advisor of the Kennedy administration as "our lieutenant, the fashionable word is 'partner,'" so let's just hear the fashionable word.

The commitment to control the world's energy resources was perfectly understandable. In fact, it reiterated a very traditional principle. One century earlier, in the 1840s, a leading policy concern of the US government was to try and gain control of the most important resources. In those days, that meant cotton. Texas was conquered (later about half of Mexico) in large part to gain a monopoly of cotton. And the point was, quite explicitly, to try to paralyze England, the superpower rival of the day (the "deterrent" force), and also to intimidate Europe. President Tyler explained that "by securing the virtual monopoly of the cotton plant," the US had acquired "a greater influence over the affairs of the world than would be found in armies however strong, or navies however numerous." "That monopoly, now secured, places all other nations at our feet," he said after the conquest. The same monopoly power neutralized British opposition to the conquest of the northwest territories and established the US in its present form. The plans of the Jacksonian Democrats were pretty much the same as those that were attributed to Saddam Hussein in the 1990s, in the most fantastic products of the propaganda system, but in that case the plan was quite realistic, in fact implemented, and very much like Washington's actual position on the primary resources of the twentieth century. Since the Second World War it has been able to implement that. So, there are very close parallels between the two episodes, and they follow the same policy concerns.

As far as oil is concerned, the US of course had – and still has – substantial oil resources of its own, and in the Gulf of Mexico under US control. North America has been a major energy producer. Venezuela was the single leading oil exporter till the 1970s, when it was surpassed by Saudi Arabia, and in 1995, Venezuela was the leading oil exporter to the US. The Woodrow Wilson administration had expelled Britain from Venezuela around 1920. The reason was that Venezuela was so rich (it had plenty of other resources too), so, no nonsense there. Saudi Arabia later replaced it, again as a virtual US colony with no interference tolerated.

Post-World War II control over the world's energy resources had another effect. It gave the US what was called "veto power" over rivals, as pointed out by George Kennan, head of the State Department planning staff and one of the leading architects of the post-World War order. He was just echoing the Jacksonian Democrats of a century earlier, whose idea was that a monopoly of cotton would give the US veto power over its rivals, primarily the British enemy, bringing them to its feet. The basic policy guidelines with regard to energy are quite interesting. They were outlined in secret by the State Department in 1944. They said that US policy must insist on "preservation of the absolute position presently obtaining" in the western hemisphere, meaning we keep total control, and therefore, "vigilant protection of existing concessions in United States hands, coupled with insistence upon the Open Door principle of equal opportunity for United States companies in new areas." Illusions aside, that's about as clear an articulation of "really existing free market doctrine" as you can have: what we have, we keep and close doors to others, and what we do not yet have, we take under the principle of the Open Door – that's the ideal market policy. In one or another form, and to various degrees, something approximating the ideal is a natural goal, domestically and everywhere else. One of the jobs of intellectuals is not to know that. So if you're looking for a job in the future, make sure you forget what I just said.

US planners were well aware of the extraordinary power in their hands – they naturally intended to use it to construct a world order which conformed to their conception of the national interest. The US, I'm now quoting, "assumed, out of self-interest, responsibility for the welfare of the world capitalist system," as put recently by respected diplomatic historian Gerald Haines, who also happens to be the senior historian of the CIA. This is quite an accurate description. There are conflicting versions of what was intended by the planners, but the most plausible version in my view is the one that they themselves articulated. The US is a very open society, with very rich documentary records, so we can learn a lot about these matters. Take George Kennan again, who was very influential. One of the primary architects of the world order, he headed the State Department policy planning staff which developed very comprehensive plans for most of the world, assigning each part of the world what was called its "function" in the new system. They were adapting plans that had been worked out during the Second World War by top planners of the State Department and the Council of Foreign Relations, which represents the more internationally-oriented sectors of the business community. They had been meeting from 1939 to 1945 in the War-Peace Studies Program. Their plans and discussions are interesting, and were largely implemented in the years that followed. There has been very little academic study of their important work, but it's there if you want to find out about it. The only serious study I know is by Lawrence Shoup and William Mintner. Kennan's position is articulated in an important planning document of 1948, which was rather comprehensive. Kennan pointed out that the US had half of the world's wealth, and that the real task is to "maintain this position of disparity" between the US and the rest of the world. He argued, therefore, that the US should put aside "unreal objectives such as human rights, the raising of the living standards, and democratization" – referring specifically to the Far East, but the point was general – and must "deal in straight power concepts" without being "hampered by idealistic slogans" and recognizing that we cannot "afford today the luxury of altruism and world-benefaction." That's another sort of thing that you immediately tend to forget, if you're looking for a job in the academic profession or in the political world. Kennan was considered too soft-hearted and sentimental for this harsh world, and he was soon replaced by Paul Nitze, who was made of sterner stuff. But his guiding principles weren't forgotten. Now, they're not studied, but they are known inside, and for that matter, they certainly weren't original at all.

A very similar conception of world order was outlined at the same time by Winston Churchill in public. He explained, in 1945, that "the government of the world must be entrusted to satisfied nations, who wished nothing more for themselves than what they had... We were like rich men dwelling at peace within their habitations," and since "our power placed us above the rest," we must use that power to keep the "hungry nations" under control and prevent them from endangering our satisfied existence. That's another principle of world order. Earlier in the century, at the peak of British power before World War I, Churchill had spelled out this realistic vision more fully to the British Cabinet. He said: "We are not a young people with an innocent record and a scanty inheritance. We have engrossed to ourselves... an altogether disproportionate share of the wealth and traffic of the world. We have got all we want in territory, and our claim to be left in the unmolested enjoyment of vast and splendid possessions, mainly acquired by violence, largely maintained by force, often seems less reasonable to others than to us." So we must teach them regular lessons in reasonableness: he was calling for an increase in the military budget. Well, the British Foreign Office recognized this was not proper fare for ordinary citizens, so that was kept secret for eighty years. Churchill understood it too: he did publish a sanitized version of this statement, but with the offending phrases removed, and one may safely assume that they will continue to be hidden away along with the equally realistic prescriptions of Kennan, and many others. One of the nice things about living in a free society is that if you are a real fanatic, if you are willing to dedicate your entire life to it, you can find out what planners are really thinking. It takes some work, but the record is there.

The more humane among the conquerors did not find the methods that were used all that reasonable. Adam Smith, for instance, bitterly condemned what he called "the savage injustice of the Europeans." He saw quite clearly that they were brutally creating the First World-Third World divide that is now so dramatic and was very much less so at that time. Smith was particularly harsh in condemning the British atrocities in Bengal, which were hardly a secret. He wasn't alone in that. Another person who chose to know was Richard Cobden, one of the rare advocates of free trade. While John Stuart Mill was explaining the need for England to conquer more of India for the benefit of the "barbarians" (and, incidentally, to gain near-monopoly control over opium so as to force its way into China and create the greatest narco-trafficking enterprise in world history), Cobden was denouncing Britain's crimes in India, and expressed his hope that the "national conscience...will be roused ere it be too late from its lethargy, and put an end to the deeds of violence and injustice which have marked every step of our progress in India." He hoped in vain. There has been no "timely atonement and reparation" for which he called, and contrary to his concerns, no "punishment due for imperial crimes." Rather, they are mostly lauded in a more attractive version of history constructed for the "satisfied nations."

Returning to the post-World War II period, there is no time to discuss what happened from 1950 to 1990. Adopting the illusions of that period, it was natural to expect that with the Cold War over, the US would at last be free to tend to the problems of the world's impoverished nations, their critical debt burdens, fragile political structures and related human rights violations, without the distortions of the East-West prism. Many prominent analysts and institutions anticipated that, for the first time in the history of imperial powers, the US would now at last be able to act with benevolence and altruism and in accord with its own true nature, which had been well-hidden for the preceding 200 years. The predictions were instantly falsified (quite standard incidentally), and the harsh policies that they deplored continued without any change, in fact even intensified as new opportunities arose.

The campaign of terror and economic warfare against Cuba is a pretty dramatic example. For about thirty years, it had been justified as self-defense against this menacing outpost of Soviet power which was ready to conquer the US. Apart from the absurdity, it's long been known that the formal decision to overthrow the government of Cuba was taken in March 1960, at a time when Castro was anti-communist, and there were no meaningful Soviet connections. With the Soviet deterrent removed in 1990, US policies became still harsher, and the ideological system didn't skip a beat. You'll have to look pretty hard to find anyone who would see the obvious, namely that the attack on Cuba became harsher with the Soviet deterrent gone – mimicking what had happened a hundred years earlier. When the British deterrent was removed, the US was finally able to conquer Cuba. It was a policy that had been proposed back in the 1820s, but the British were in the way. That was no longer true at the end of the nineteenth century, so the US intervened to prevent Cubans from liberating themselves from Spain, and then took Cuba over, granting it "independence," but in effect as a virtual US colony and plantation. And now again, with the Russian deterrent gone the policies became harsher – the opposite of the predictions – in accord with the way world order actually works.

As for the problems of the world's impoverished nations, Washington did turn its attention to them but not quite in the manner that had been predicted. Rather, it did so by slashing its aid program, which was already the most miserly in the developed world. The timing was elegant. Congress passed legislation slashing support for the poor on the day the UNICEF press conference released its 1995 report, which estimated that 13 million children die each year from easily treatable diseases and malnutrition that could be dealt with for pennies a day (that's an increase of 2 million since their previous report). It's a "silent genocide" (as the head of the World Health Organization called it), which can now be intensified, with the propaganda needs of the Cold War gone, under what's now conventionally called "donor fatigue." None of this is a problem for the doctrinal institutions. And so it continues, on and on.

Nothing substantial changed after the Cold War, exactly as a serious person would have expected, except that things got harsher because there were new possibilities. In the real world, the perceived task of the US remained as it had been in 1945, when it "assumed, out of self-interest, responsibility for the welfare of the world capitalist system," as Haines described, though there were now new contingencies that required different tactics. After the Cold War, as before, planners acted on the basis of rational thinking and also historical experience as they saw it. It's important to remember one aspect of the historical experience which was so conventional among states and other power systems that it's a virtual cliché, namely the doctrine that our preponderance of power is both our right and our need. It's a right because of our nobility, which is unique in history, and it's our need because we are surrounded by fiendish enemies who are bent on our destruction. That's close to a universal principle of the educated classes, so of course it applied in this case. It happens to be deeply rooted in US history from the early cleansing of the continent to the present, and too familiar here and elsewhere to require elaboration. And of course, no US innovation.

Another highly relevant aspect of the historical experience is perhaps less familiar than it should be. It bears on India and most of the world. I am referring to the fact that from its origins, the US has been "the mother country and bastion of modern protectionism." I am quoting the eminent economic historian Paul Bairoch, who proceeds to document his more general conclusion that "it is difficult to find another case where the facts so contradict a dominant theory" as the doctrine that free markets were the engine of growth, or, for that matter, that the powerful adhere to their principles except for temporary advantage.

The fact that the so-called late developers have departed from market principles has been quite familiar to economic historians at least, certainly since the work of Alexander Gershenkron some years ago. The same is also true of early developers. The US had always been extreme, from its origins, in rejecting market discipline. That's how it developed in the first place, beginning with textiles and then on to steel, energy, chemicals, computers and electronics, pharmaceuticals and biotechnology, agribusiness, in fact every sector of the functioning economy, and gained enormous wealth and power; instead of pursuing its comparative advantage in the export of furs, as the doctrines of economic rationality would have dictated – doctrines that were taught to the rest of the world by force.

The American developmental state broke no new ground at all. Britain had done exactly the same thing. They did turn to free trade in 1846, after 150 years of protectionism had given them such an enormous advantage that a "level playing field" seemed a pretty safe bet, and even then continuing to rely on the fact that forty percent of its exports could go to the Third World, which means mostly their colonial world. For British textiles, for instance, the biggest export market was India, not because India was unable to develop its own textile industry or shipbuilding or steel or other industries, but because imperial force simply barred the way. The same was true in Egypt and elsewhere. During the era of railway building (the latter part of the last century), the US steel industry boomed, relying in no small measure on the fact that tariffs were so prohibitive that higher-quality and cheaper British goods could be kept out. In addition to that, there were military contracts and other state subsidies. Not in India, however, even though Indian production of iron had matched that of western Europe a century earlier, and Indian steel-making for shipbuilding and military production was more advanced than Britain as late as the 1820s, when British engineers were studying Indian techniques to try to close the technological gap.

One may note, in passing, that there are many contemporary analogues. The Reaganites, noted for their exalted free market rhetoric, were in fact the most protectionist administration in postwar US history, virtually doubling import restrictions, and also pouring public funds into high-tech industry, often under the traditional cover of "defense." The goal was to "reindustrialize America," which was falling behind Japan (and Germany) because American management had failed to understand their new efficient production techniques. To help overcome the gap, the Reaganites again turned to the military, as conventionally in the past, setting up a program of "Management Technology" in which the technological gap was studied and management was brought up to date at public expense, one of many such mechanisms.

Returning to nineteenth-century India, Britain spent vast sums on railway projects in India, favoring those expenditures over irrigation and agricultural improvement, but with little linkage effect for the Indian economy. Railway engines were produced in Bombay at that time at reasonable cost, but they were imported from England instead, not by the choice of Indians. Later, British steel was completely priced out of the international market, but the imperial preference system kept the Indian market and others open, while what were called discriminating protection principles denied similar support to Indian industry. All that was on the altar of free trade, a conveniently flexible doctrine.

It can hardly escape notice that outside of Europe the only countries that developed are those that escaped the rule of Europe. The first one was the US, later it was Japan and some of its own colonies – it's not easy to find an exception. It's true from the origins of Europe's industrial revolution, when Daniel Defoe, expressing a common perception in 1728, warned that England faced an uphill struggle in attempting to compete with China and India, which have "the most extended Manufacture, and the greatest variety in the World; and their Manufactures push themselves upon the World, by the mere Stress of their Cheapness." So naturally protection and violence were necessary to overcome those unfair advantages. The more advanced countries in Asia might also have had the highest real wages in the world, at the time, and the best conditions for working class organization, so the most detailed recent scholarship indicates, contrary to long-standing beliefs. "Britain itself would have been de-industrialized by the cheapness of Indian calicoes, if protectionist policies had not been adopted," concludes the same work, a very interesting PhD dissertation at Harvard by Prasannan Parthasarathi. And that extends to other industries as well. England faced the same problems in China in the mid-nineteenth century, overcoming them by the vicious Opium Wars, right at about the time of England's worst atrocities in India.

Defiance of market principles has always been a significant factor in economic development. That includes the post-World War II period. For instance, Europe, Japan, and the newly industrializing countries on its periphery all received a crucial economic stimulus from US military adventures. US military Keynesianism probably had a larger effect in revitalizing European economies than the Marshall plan, some political economists argue. The postwar Japanese economy was stagnant until the Korean War gave it a big shot in the arm. The Vietnam War did the same for Japan and for South Korea as well. Today's First and Third Worlds, as I said, were much more alike in the eighteenth century. One reason for the enormous difference between them today is that the rulers were in a position to avoid the market discipline that they rammed down the throat of their dependencies. Bairoch, in his own study, concludes that the compulsory economic liberalism forced on the colonies in the nineteenth century is a major element in explaining the delay in their industrialization. Sometimes, in fact, it was de-industrialization, as in the Indian case. That's a story that continues into the present under various guises, often with the cooperation of elite elements in Third World countries; because however much their countries may suffer they themselves benefit. These approaches do lead to highly stratified societies, in which some sectors do very well. Bairoch and other economic historians have studied these matters extensively.

Economists don't pay much attention to it, but in economic history itself it's pretty well known.

Economic theory considerably understates the role of state intervention for the wealthy. One reason is that attention is focused on a very narrow category of market interference. If you look at the studies, you see only the study of protectionism, but that's only one form of market interference and not necessarily the most important one. Just to mention one kind of obvious omission, the industrial revolution in Britain and the US was fuelled by cheap cotton. What made cotton cheap was the violent elimination of the indigenous population of the southeast US and bringing in slaves – neither of these actions exactly an attribute of market orthodoxy. But that's not counted when one talks about market interferences. The crucial matter of control of energy, that I mentioned, is another example. And so the story continues to the present. It's rather striking in Bairoch's history, not just because he is a very distinguished economic historian, but because it's a very good history. He limits himself to protectionist measures and concludes, therefore, that after the Second World War, the US at least moved towards liberal internationalism, after a long history of leading the way in violating these principles, including in its most rapid growth periods. And there is an element of truth in this picture. The truth is that leading sectors of the US economy, particularly the more capital-intensive sectors, high-tech industry and the financial sector, did come to favor the liberal international principles from around the middle of the century for much the same reasons that motivated their British predecessors a century earlier: it looked like they could win any competition, so let's have free competition. But that picture is seriously misleading, because it's far too narrowly focused. American business leaders had learned a very important lesson from the enormous success of the semi-command economy during World War II. The lesson was that state subsidy and coordination could preserve and expand the system of private profit. That lesson was taught to the right people – the corporate executives who flocked to Washington to run the war-time economy. They haven't forgotten it since. By the late 1940s, the business world recognized quite frankly that high-tech industry could not survive in a free enterprise economy, and that the government had to be what was called "the savior." For quite convincing reasons, having to do more with power than efficiency, military Keynesianism was much preferred to alternatives, one reason being that it was much easier to sell, as the first Secretary of the Air Force, Stuart Symington (a liberal Democrat), pointed out to Congress. He said the word to use is not "subsidy," the word to use is "security," and so it remains. You don't tell people that they are paying their taxes to the rich. What you tell them is that you are in danger of being destroyed, so you have to put your money in the pockets of the rich – indirectly, by processes you don't see and are not publicly discussed, though anyone involved in science, technology, and the business world knows them very well from first-hand experience.

There is hardly a sector of the functioning economy that doesn't rely very heavily on these measures. That's one of the main reasons why the Pentagon budget today remains roughly at Cold War levels. In fact, it is increasing – not because any danger is increasing but because it's needed. I should say that my friends in the disarmament movement, I think, have sometimes misled people by writing about how many schools we could build if we didn't have so many jet planes, and so on. Sure, that's true. The business world understood that perfectly well back in the 1940s and even wrote about it. But they want the jet planes and not the schools, because that's the way you get public funding for metallurgy and avionics and the aeronautical industry, and so on and so forth. There are fluctuations to be sure, and the statist reactionaries of the Reagan years, as I mentioned, broke new records for protectionism and public subsidy. They also boasted about it quite frankly to the business audience. And while the free trade enthusiasts and fiscal conservatives were preaching economic liberalism to everyone else (including the general population at home), they doubled import restrictions, increased public subsidies to the rich and shifted wealth to them by fiscal and other policies, while also undermining the labor movement, and also quickly transformed the world's leading creditor into its leading debtor, again for reasons having to do with power – not efficiency. If the Reaganites had permitted market forces to function in the 1980s, there would probably be no steel or automobile industries in the US today, nor machine tools or semiconductors or automation or robotics, or much else. The Reagan administration effectively closed the door to Japanese competition and poured in plenty of public funds under the usual guise of security. No such measures were needed to safeguard the leading civilian export industry, namely aircraft, or the huge and profitable tourism industry, which is aircraft-based. These are largely an offshoot of the Pentagon system, which is by far the most important component of the welfare state, I mean in terms of magnitude (now growing at the hands of still more fanatical fiscal conservatives).

Well, if economics and economic history didn't have such a narrow focus, these would be primary topics of investigation, and if you look at them it's simply not true that the US turned to liberal internationalism after 1945. It did it in a highly selective manner, with plenty of state subsidy and support at home under the guise of defense. And given all this, it is entirely natural that, say, when Bill Clinton showed up at the Asia-Pacific economic conference in Seattle back in 1993, and described his grand vision of the free market future, he did it in the hangar of the Boeing corporation and selected Boeing as the model for this grand market of the future. This makes perfect sense, you could hardly find a finer prototype of the publicly-subsidized private-profit economy that's called free enterprise. Boeing is a publicly created and publicly subsidized enterprise, and it is indeed the country's leading civilian exporter, but that's because what it exports (the planes you fly in, including the one I just came here on) are modifications of military design, with the electronics and the avionics and the metallurgy and much else paid for by the public, under the guise of security – in much earlier years. Equally important was Clinton's prime illustration of the miracles of the market at the Jakarta session a year later, namely Exxon, another stellar example of entrepreneurial value which won a 35 billion dollar contract to develop natural gas fields in Indonesia. Incidentally, that was called "jobs for Americans," and sure there were some US managers and some skilled workers and a few others. Exxon's stocks shot up right after that, because of the great joy built up by the prospect of the new jobs for Americans. "Jobs" has become the technical term for "profits": it's considered improper to mention the word "profits" in public discourse, so you say "jobs" instead and the important people understand that it means profits.

All these victories for free market capitalism elicited great awe and acclaim, as one would expect of a well-behaved society. Equally natural is the fact that Newt Gingrich, head of the conservative revolution who preaches what's called "tough love" to the weak and the destitute, is also the country's leading welfare enthusiast. He brings more federal subsidies to his wealthy constituents than any comparable district in the country. And that contradiction poses no problem, passes with, at most, occasional mention. The reason is that both political parties, as well as respectable opinion generally, are committed to the same doctrine, the same double-edged conception of the free market, namely market discipline is just right for the poor at home, the defenseless Third World and everybody else, but the wealthy have to be protected. That's a principle of world order that goes back a couple of hundred years, and it's not going to change.

I should stress that there is nothing special about the US. In this respect, the reliance on state power is quite general. If you want an example of what's misleadingly called capitalism, here is one from the London *Financial Times*, one of the world's leading business newspapers. A couple of days ago, it had a review of a new study of the top 100 global corporations in the *Fortune* list. It found that, out of 100, all had benefited from industrial and trade policies of their national governments, and at least twenty would not have survived if they had not been saved outright by government intervention. That's what is called "capitalism." Meanwhile, everybody else has to endure market discipline, because real science tells us that.

Now, this historical dedication to protectionism and state power, and these remarkable successes of military Keynesianism during World War II, provided a good part of the intellectual equipment of the architects of the new world order of 1945. That remains true of those who are reshaping the system today, both domestically and internationally, under some new conditions. Going back to the postwar era, the first task was to restore the industrial societies with their traditional order pretty much intact. That meant restoring Nazi and fascist collaborators in the business community, and marginalizing and dispersing the anti-fascist resistance. This was often done with considerable violence. In South Korea, about 100,000 people were killed before what's called the Korean War; they were mostly the anti-fascist resistance forces. The American occupying army actually used Japanese police forces to help, as well as collaborators. The same is true in many other places.

The second task, closely related to the first, was to assign to the various parts of the South what were called their "functions" in the service of these goals. The guidelines were pretty much the same as outlined by Kennan and Churchill, and they remained very stable. If you look at high-level planning documents, the primary threat to US interests is consistently depicted as what are called "radical" and "nationalist" regimes that are responsive to popular pressure for "immediate improvements in the low living standards of the masses" and development for domestic needs. That's called "radical nationalism," or sometimes "economic nationalism," and these tendencies conflict with the demand for a "political and economic climate conducive to private investment" with adequate repatriation of profits and "protection of our raw materials" – "our" raw materials, which by accident happen to be somewhere else. Opposition to economic nationalism was kind of a reflex (when it came to other countries, of course, not at home, where we have an extreme form of economic nationalism). Britain agreed. So the British Foreign

Office, in 1949, feared that the fall of China might lead to a type of economy in which there was no place for the foreign manufacturer, the foreign banker, the foreign trader – which is of course an unacceptable outcome.

US planning principles were most clearly illustrated in Latin America, where there was no interference, and US planners could do what they wanted. So there the values and ideals and goals come out with considerable clarity. In February 1945, the US called a hemispheric conference, where it presented the "economic charter of the Americas." Its basic principle was the elimination of economic nationalism "in all its forms." That was a problem because, as the State Department recognized, all of Latin America was overcome at the time with what was called "the philosophy of the new nationalism," which "embraces policies designed to bring about a broader distribution of wealth and to raise the standard of living of the masses." Furthermore, "Latin Americans are convinced that the first beneficiaries of the development of a country's resources should be the people of that country." Accordingly, they had to be instructed in the principles of economic rationality, which dictate that the first beneficiaries of a country's resources are the US investors. Latin America was supposed to provide resources, markets, investment opportunities, cheap labor and all that sort of thing, but it was not to undergo what Washington called "excessive industrial development." Both the Truman and the Eisenhower administrations allowed only what was called "complementary development." So for instance, Brazil would be permitted to produce steel, but only the kind that US industry was interested in (you know, cheap, labor-intensive steel). And as far as possible, the principle was extended to the whole world. It is the basis for aid programs and so on: only complementary development, not the kind of development that would interfere with US-based private power.

Of course, Washington's position prevailed at the hemispheric conference – a major reason why Latin America has the highest inequality in the world and has been a political and socio-economic disaster for the vast majority of the population. These consistent disasters are particularly instructive when we recall that this is an area with very rich resources and potential. The region faces no external threat – it's had the benefit of close supervision by the worlds' richest and most powerful country, which was establishing what are called "testing areas for scientific methods of development" and "showcases for democracy and capitalism." It has had repeated "economic miracles," including in the two major economies of the region. Brazil up to six years ago and Mexico until December 1994 were both heralded as success stories for American-style capitalism until the (standard) collapse of the economic miracle, at which point the same measures that were hailed as proof of the marvels of capitalism become proof of the statist deviation from market principles, if not Marxism. The miracles have indeed been miraculous at least for some, at least for US investors and for Latin American elites who live in tremendous luxury. Meanwhile, the general population has sunk deeper into misery and despair. In large measure, this is because of the ways in which Latin America was opened to international markets, and the internal policies that result in part from the historical rapacity of Latin American elites and in part from external pressures.

If we compare Latin America with East Asia, there are a lot of differences, so I don't want to be too glib about it, but some differences are striking. They developed more or less along the same lines till around 1980, when they split very sharply. Latin America entered into a huge fiscal crisis, a debt crisis, and so on. East Asia keeps developing. Why? Well, there are some striking differences. There's an enormous capital flight from Latin America – it's open to international markets, and the wealthy are quite free to export capital. If Latin Americans could control the wealthy they wouldn't have a debt crisis. That's not a problem in East Asia. There the state is powerful enough to control capital as well as labor, which it controls everywhere. In South Korea, you could theoretically get the death penalty for capital flight, and there wasn't any capital flight. That's not necessarily a feature of autocratic societies. Britain has instituted similar measures against capital flight several times, including after the Second World War (in accord with the Bretton Woods principles of the postwar economic order, and also the IMF rules, still technically in effect). But Latin America didn't have that advantage. It's open to international markets. Another factor is this tremendous inequality, much worse than East Asia, which means lots and lots of luxury imports – plenty of Mercedes-Benz are coming in, and those sorts of things. That means huge imports, and huge trade deficits, and so on. These two factors are a big part of the crisis out there – just a simple consequence of a particular form of openness to international markets.

These very same scientific methods that brought those results in Latin America are now being applied in much of eastern Europe, with similar effects. There's a lot of puzzlement in the West over the fact that most of the population of Russia and even the former empire appear to be looking back at the pre-reform period (as it is called) as a kind of a golden age. There's a lot of talk about why that is – you know, perhaps the past looks better as it recedes into the background, they forget what it was, or something like that. I don't think that's what is happening. There isn't much yearning to return to Stalin's dungeon either. It's not so much that they see something receding, as something approaching. What they see approaching is Brazil and Mexico. Awful as the Soviet system was, what the US and its European allies imposed on the Third World was an even worse monstrosity, and the restored eastern European Third World is coming to learn that lesson.

Back to 1945, other parts of the world were also assigned their roles. Southeast Asia, according to the Kennan policy planning studies, was to fulfill its main function as a service area for the reconstruction of western industrial capitalism that now included Japan. Japan was to be granted its new order in East Asia, what Kennan called the "empire toward the south," all now safely under US control. Independent nationalism had to be demolished for the usual reasons, as was done with usual brutality and power. Africa, the US didn't much care about, it didn't count much. It was, therefore, to be handed over to Europe to "exploit," as Kennan put it, for the reconstruction of Europe. He also thought that exploiting Africa would give Europe a kind of psychological shot in the arm, which they needed, being sort of gloomy in those days. You could imagine a different relation between Europe and Africa, but that never occurred to anyone; all this has been public for many years, but there's no comment about it. As for the Middle East, it was to be incorporated directly within the US system. The local management of the Middle East was to be assigned to the British in those days, with what in earlier days Britain and the US called "an Arab façade," submissive family dictatorships that would ensure that the huge profits from oil flow primarily to the West (mainly the US and Britain), not to the people of the region. That's their crucial job (they are permitted to live in super-luxury themselves, a common feature of dependencies under imperial rule as well). If they don't carry out their jobs, they're out of the window; if they do, they can be as brutal as they want. The US also has to keep its finger on the nozzle, for reasons I mentioned.

As for South Asia, it was not a major area of US planning concern, so the documentary record indicates. There the primary concern was to prevent what Kennan called "infection" from a potentially communist Indonesia or China. In 1948, these processes were taken very seriously. So seriously that, in 1948, Kennan considered Indonesia to be the primary problem facing US policy in the world. It was a judgment reiterated by the Eisenhower government a decade later. Eisenhower identified three major crisis areas in the world. One was Indonesia, another was North Africa, and the third was the Middle East – all oil producers, all Islamic, though then secular. The fear about Indonesia was that advocates of independent development might win a political victory. That meant the one mass political party, namely the PKI (the Indonesian Communist Party). And Indonesia specialists these days consider this possibility not at all unrealistic. One of the leading specialists is the Australian scholar Harold Crouch, who wrote the standard book for the period. He writes that "the PKI had won widespread support not as a revolutionary party but as an organization defending the interests of the poor within the existing system," developing a "mass base among the peasantry" through its "vigor in defending the interests of the... poor." American internal documents for that period have been released recently (very selectively). They reveal great fear that the democratic processes, if allowed to function, would come out the wrong way, so they had to be stopped. First, they were stopped by a huge campaign of CIA subversion and support for civil rebellion in the outer Islands, in 1958. They were finally terminated by the huge slaughter in 1965 of hundreds of thousands, maybe a million people, mostly landless peasants. The one mass-based political party, the PKI, was finally destroyed, and an end was put to the danger of democracy in Indonesia. That slaughter elicited enormous euphoria in the West – you have to read it to believe it.

Similar fears lie behind the US attack on South Vietnam, later all of Indochina, and the overthrow of parliamentary governments in Guatemala and Brazil and Chile and a lot more. None of these involved any meaningful security threat from Russia or China, though that was the reflexive pretext by the government and commentariat. Radical and nationalistic regimes are intolerable in themselves, even more so if they seem to be succeeding in terms that might be meaningful to other people facing similar problems. In that case, they become what Kissinger termed viruses that can infect others, or as Acheson put it, they become "rotten apples that might spoil the barrel." For the public, they are "dominoes" that are going to topple by aggression and conquest. Internally the absurdity of this picture is often conceded, and the real threat is recognized. When Henry Kissinger moaned that the contagious example of Chile would infect not only Latin America but also southern Europe, he didn't really anticipate that Allende's hordes were going to descend on Rome, but rather that Chile's example would send Italian voters the wrong message – namely that democratic social reform was a possible option. The same is true quite generally. When you detect a virus, you take action to destroy it, and potential victims have to be immunized: typically, by state repression and terror. That pattern repeats itself over and over again through the years. It continues without notable change after the Cold War – that's a substantial core element of modern history.

Take a look at the Cold War itself. What's that? Well, to a large extent it falls into the very same pattern. The Bolshevik Revolution, in 1917, extricated the Soviet Union from the western-dominated periphery (remember that this was the original Third World, going back to the fifteenth century in pre-Columbian times), and it set off the inevitable reaction, beginning with instant military intervention. From the outset, those have been basic elements of the Cold War. The underlying logic was not fundamentally different from Guatemala or Grenada. Of course, the scale of the problem was enormously different. So Grenada you can take care of over the weekend. The Soviet Union is a different story. It took seventy years. Bolshevik Russia was what is called radical nationalist – communist in the technical sense – unwilling "to complement the industrial economies of the West," in the semi-official phrase which I am quoting. In fact, it was no more communist or socialist than it was democratic, in the literal sense of these terms, and furthermore there were no conceivable military threats. The Bolshevik example did have undeniable appeal, not only in the Third World but even in the rich societies. That was a fact that very greatly concerned Woodrow Wilson and Lloyd George at that time, as we now know from released records, and it continued to be a concern right into the 1960s (that's when the documentary record runs dry). At this point, Kennedy and Macmillan are discussing the danger that Russian success will be just too influential for others. In short, the Soviet Union was a gigantic rotten apple. It wasn't Stalin's monstrous crimes that bothered western leaders, any more than in the case of Mussolini or Hitler or others who got plenty of support till they stepped out of line (Saddam Hussein is a recent case). Truman liked and admired Stalin. So did Churchill. Right through the Yalta conference Churchill was defending Stalin in internal discussions at the British Cabinet. Truman felt that the United States would have no problem whatsoever with the bloodthirsty tyrant if the US were to get its way eighty-five percent of the time. Well, it couldn't get that – so the virus had to be destroyed. The ultra-nationalist threat was greatly enhanced after Russia's leading role in defeating Hitler left it in control of eastern Europe, separating these regions too from the domains of western control – again those are traditional Third World resource, market, and investment areas for western Europe. In this case, the rotten apple was so huge (and after the World War so militarily powerful too) and the virus was so dangerous that this particular facet of the North-South conflict took on a life of its own from the very outset. And in my view that's the major character of the Cold War.

Similar concerns drove US policies in South Asia. There is one comprehensive scholarly study of this, a very good one by Robert McMahon, running through recently released documents. His conclusion, that of a very conservative scholar, is that western policies are what brought the Cold War to Asia – destroying Nehru's vision of a zone of peace. Pakistan was set up as a military base, in large part as a component of the regional enforcement system directed at the Middle East. McMahon does keep to the conventional doctrine that US policy was "driven not by pursuit of material gain or geopolitical advantage as the policies of so many expansionist powers of the past had been," but rather by "largely illusory military strategic and psychological fears." Curiously, the same foolish and unnecessary errors were made everywhere in the world, under the same illusory fears that go from the terrifying threat of Grenada or Nicaragua to panic about Ho Chi Minh setting off on a world conquest and so on. The real concern that McMahon's work points to was that China might win the economic competition with India, thus discrediting the capitalist democratic path of development. In fact, what he calls Washington's irrational sense of insecurity, when you look at it case by case, turns out to be the perfectly rational concern that unless the world is totally under control, the rotten apples may spread unwanted messages, and the interests of the real rulers may be damaged, if only slightly. It's an interesting fact about the intellectual culture (in the United States and Britain and most of the world to my knowledge) that highly consistent actions that prove very successful for their designers are consistently criticized in retrospect as foolish and naive and based on illusory fears. Apparently, it's more acceptable to attribute to the planners consistent irrationality, verging on literal insanity, than it is to recognize the truth of the principles enunciated by Churchill and Kennan and others, at least in internal documents where they are, in fact, particularly well-articulated.

With the Cold War over, things continue pretty much as before. Eastern Europe is being driven back to its earlier status. Parts that belonged before to the industrial West, like the Czech Republic and western Poland, are pretty much returning to that status. Others are drifting back towards something resembling their Third World origins, as illustrated by economic and social indicators. Just to mention one, the number of extra deaths in Russia alone is estimated at over half a million a year by 1993; that's rather successful killing as a result of the capitalist reforms that were instituted in 1989 (this is from a study by UNICEF, which supports the so-called reforms). This picture is very easily recognized by anyone familiar with Brazil and Mexico and so on, and will doubtless be lauded as another economic miracle, as indeed it will be to the people who count.

A few months after the fall of the Berlin Wall, the White House submitted its annual request to the Congress for the military budget. The text had been the same for years – we need a huge military budget because of the Russians. One thing has changed – the reason. It was no longer the awesome Russian threat that required enormous expenditures for what was called the "defense industrial base" and the intervention forces aimed primarily at the Middle East. Rather, it was frankly conceded that in the Middle East the threats to US interests "could not be laid at the Kremlin's door" (contrary to many lies now withdrawn, no longer being serviceable), and it turns out that the general threat that required the United States to spend as much on the military as the rest of the world combined was the "technological sophistication" of Third World powers. That's what the threat is, which the US is incidentally trying to increase as much at it can by being the largest arms seller in the world, which of course means that we are facing potential threats for which we need more arms to protect ourselves, and so on. None of this elicits any ridicule. In fact, it didn't even elicit news report or comment. So everything proceeds on course, which isn't at all surprising when you think about the real character of the Cold War.

If you want to determine the true nature of the Cold War, it's a useful idea to ask a simple question. Take a look at the end and ask who's cheering and who's despairing. That tells you something about the real nature of the conflict. So let's try it in this case. The Cold War is over – who's cheering? Well, in the East there are some people cheering – the old Communist Party hierarchy. They are extremely happy; they're now taking on the standard role of the highly privileged elite that cooperates with western power. They're called the capitalists – rich beyond their wildest dreams – and they won the Cold War. So the communist party leadership, they're the winners. Among the losers are the general population, sinking into typical Third World misery and dreaming vainly of the days before they rejoined the

Third World. They were doubtless released from tyranny, and are grateful at least for that. So, that tells you who won and who lost in the East. Who won and who lost in the West? There are very large cheers from investors, who regained their privileged access to the economy of the former Soviet empire – markets, investment opportunities, cheap labor, the whole business. The international business press, incidentally, is very frank about this. Surveying the wreckage, the London *Financial Times* had a report headlined "Green Shoots in Communism's Ruins," meaning everything is pretty rotten but there are a couple of good things. Green shoots turn out to be new opportunities for western corporations, now that the capitalist reforms have caused "rising unemployment and pauperization of large sections of the industrial working class." That means a submissive and disciplined labor force is available (also healthy and educated, so things have changed from the days when eastern Europe was a typical Third World service area for the West). They're willing to work longer hours than what the *Financial Times* calls the "pampered" western workers, at much lower wages and with much fewer benefits, and that's kept that way by the very tough anti-labor policies of these repressive neo-liberal states. General Motors, Benz and others now have a new weapon to use against the pampered workers at home, who will have to abandon their "luxurious lifestyles," the business press tells us cheerily. Once again, that tells you who won and who lost the Cold War. In the West, the ones who lost are the pampered western workers who now have a new weapon against them – meaning most of the population. They lost the Cold War. Those who won the Cold War are the executives and investors of Benz, General Motors, and the rest. That tells you not only what it was about to a large extent, but also why everything else persists.

I should add that as elsewhere western investors in eastern Europe understand the free market as they always did. So General Motors and Benz and the rest will invest there, but they'll demand tax holidays, stiff tariffs to ensure market control and the usual amenities, leaving the new Third World countries with the debts, and the pollution, and the task of providing infrastructure, and all that stuff. Benz recently worked out a similar deal with the state of Alabama, southeast United States, which indeed does offer something like Third World conditions, structurally speaking.

Well, there certainly have been important changes in world order – I'll finish briefly with these. One of the biggest changes was deregulation of financial markets. Back in the early 1970s, that was a primary factor in the huge explosion of speculative financial transactions and manipulations (speculation against currencies, things like that), which now constitute about ninety-five percent of foreign exchange transactions. According to a recent UNCTAD (United Nations Conference on Trade and Development) report, it was ten percent of a far smaller total in 1970. That's a very radical change, and those consequences were understood right off. In 1978, James Tobin, a Nobel Prize-winning economist, pointed out (in his presidential address to the American Economic Association) that these changes (then just beginning) were going to drive the world towards a low-wage, low-growth equilibrium and also high profits. A recent study, which was directed by Paul Volcker (head of the Federal Reserve), attributes about half of the slowdown of growth since the early 1970s to just this factor. When capital is not being used for investment and commerce, but is being used for speculation against currencies and so on, this drives down growth in several ways. For one, capital is withdrawn from productive uses. For another, it's a weapon against stimulative policy. If any government, even in a country like the United States, tries to do something to stimulate the economy and increase growth, which threatens to bring with it inflation and so on, there's the threat of huge capital flight, which is not trivial with a trillion dollars moving across financial markets on an average day. That's a powerful weapon even against the US, certainly against any Third World country. And it's a major factor in the attack against democracy, since national economic planning becomes much harder, even if populations can get some control over their own governments in some fashion.

There have been other developments that contribute to these tendencies. The telecommunications revolution took place around the same time (that's another offshoot of the state system), and of course it facilitated the globalization of industry and finance. It made it possible for corporate headquarters to be in New York, financial operations in some tax haven, and production wherever people can be beaten down most efficiently (say Indonesia, where wages are about half the level of China – it's called an economic miracle too). Corporate executives have also learned that this new information technology allows much more effective command and control, *BusinessWeek* reports, failing to add that the same technology differently used could radically reduce superfluous layers of management and devolve decision-making to working people. If you look at the history of automation, which has been well studied, it was so inefficient that it was developed through the state system (the Air Force for instance); but after decades of development, it was handed over to industry for private profit. That's standard. But the point here is that the way it was developed was not in the interests of economic efficiency, but in the interest of power: automation could have been used to put decision-making power into the hands of (let's say) skilled machinists and eliminate management; or it could be used to intensify management control and to deskill machinists. The second way was adopted in the state system for reasons of power and class war and not economic efficiency. One of the nice things about the state system is that you can do that without anyone knowing about it (unless they happen to have read David Noble's fine study of the topic). Also, you don't have to worry about costs as the public is paying for it. And the same is true of the telecommunication systems that are allowing for more effective command and control.

The end of the Cold War contributed to these tendencies, as I mentioned, by adding new weapons to the armory, and by reducing the slight space that was available for non-alignment and independence in the Third World. A new version of the world order is taking shape. It has effective power transferred, to an unprecedented extent, to private tyrannies that are internally immune to the threat of democracy and generally unaccountable. Along with democracy, markets also are under attack, even if we put aside the massive state intervention. Increasing economic concentration offers endless devices to evade and undermine market discipline. Just to mention one aspect: about forty percent of what's called world trade is actually not trade at all in any meaningful sense – its intra-firm, like a single corporation shipping something somewhere else and then shipping it back, never entering anybody's market. This is called "trade" because it has to cross international borders – that's forty percent of world trade, and over fifty percent of trade for the US and Japan. These, of course, are estimates; investigating private tyrannies is no easy matter. Operations internal to corporations are carefully managed by a very visible hand and they offer all sorts of mechanisms to undermine market discipline, leading to what's properly being called a system of "corporate mercantilism" in the international arena. That system is rife with the kinds of conspiracies of the "masters of mankind" which Adam Smith warned against, not to speak of the traditional reliance on state power and public subsidy, and it's pretty well recognized. Today, *BusinessWeek* perceives what they call a mega-corporate state in which there will be a few global firms within particular economic sectors. The vast majority of the world's population is supposed to be subjected to market discipline and be told how wonderful it is. They are not supposed to hear things like this – this is for the readers of the business press and people who care about running the world.

Well, that partly skims the surface. It's pretty easy to see why the masters now perceive a real hope of achieving the kind of end of history that they've often announced in the past (always wrongly so far). It is also easy to see the reasons for the mood of anxiety and hopelessness that prevails in every part of the world, including the industrial societies, although there are also many signs of resistance all over the place, and I think they offer plenty of hope. It's certainly possible to reverse this course. Human institutions and human decisions made within them are not engraved in stone, and there are ways to change them. You have to penetrate the clouds of deceit and distortion; you have to learn the truth about the world, to organize, to act, to change. It's never been easy, it's never been impossible. There are new challenges now, as well as new possibilities of international solidarity that weren't there before. There's rarely been a time in history when the choice of whether to undertake these struggles carried such fateful human consequences.

Question and Answer Session

Question*: There is a wide gulf between the First World and the Third World, and the aim of the Bush team is to sustain and perpetuate US hegemony. What are the prospects for alliances among nationalities of the Third World to break this hegemony?*

Chomsky: Well, there are plenty of opportunities for solidarity within the South, but it's important to recognize other things that are going on. One of the striking features of this world order is the extension to industrial societies of something like the Third World model. So the US is also being subjected to a kind of structural adjustment, and the same with England. More and more of these rich countries are taking on the look of Third World countries: highly stratified, with a superfluous population, the usual picture. And that creates both a need and a possibility for alliances that cross the traditional North-South divide – because a good part of the population of the North is becoming like the South, at a different absolute level but in structural terms. That is beginning to happen, and I think it's offering promising avenues for international solidarity. So, for the first time ever, there has been cooperation, for example, between North American and Central American labor. The US unions have traditionally opposed the Central American labor unions (and even supported brutal attacks on them), but now they are supporting them and sometimes doing pretty effective work in solidarity with working people in Central America. Indeed, they have common interests, and that extends over the whole world. General Motors can move not only to Mexico but to Poland, and this means that the reaction to this form of tyranny also has to be international. It calls for popular internationals of a kind that hasn't existed for a long time, and in fact never really existed. I think the prospects for that are unprecedented. The same kind of technology (like telecommunications and so on) that allows centralized control also facilitates the spread of information and common action among people who want to resist it. And after all, the powers we face are very fragile. Take, say, corporations. Corporations exist on the basis of an extremely thin reed. In the US, they are given charters, charters that can be revoked. And they can be eliminated by simple parliamentary decisions – parliamentary decisions that could be part of major changes in the whole structure of the world order. Nothing like this would be easy, but the main reason why it's not easy is that people don't understand the power they have in their hands. I think that's the hard thing to overcome, and it is within reach. That can be changed, not only internally within the Third World, but also across North-South borders.

Question: *Why do you think that the world order is maintained only by physical powers, like military and economic power? What about spiritual powers (not necessarily religious)?*

Chomsky: I think it's quite right, that these powers help to maintain world order. I agree with that very strongly. In fact, this point has been understood for a long time. It was explained rather nicely by one of my favorite figures, David Hume – a very conservative, very smart analyst, a contemporary of Adam Smith and a friend of his. He wrote down the principles of government. The first principle he introduced by talking about what he regarded as a paradox of government. The paradox, as he put it, is that "force is in the hands of the governed," not the governors. He said that's true of most societies, even the most authoritarian ones. From totalitarian societies to free societies, force is in the hands of the governed, and that's the paradox – how come they don't throw out their rulers, who are oppressing them? Well, the answer must be that power rests, in part, on the control of opinion. It is by opinion only that the population is controlled, he argued – that's spiritual power. That means imposing a range of hopes, and aspirations, and assumptions, and goals, and so on that keep people from acting to overthrow the powers that are oppressing them. Because force is indeed in the hands of the governed, there is no doubt about that. So the US, which is in many ways the freest society in the world, is also the one where the most effort is put into controlling opinion. That costs about a trillion dollars a year in just plain marketing, which is not only a means of creating artificial wants, but also a big device of control. So is state propaganda. The business world has understood for a long time that the public mind is the major threat facing corporate power. The US has a huge public relations industry, which is designed to control thought and attitudes, and its leaders are very frank about it. They have to fight what they call "the everlasting battle for the minds of men," indoctrinate people with the capitalist story and so on. Those are very strong techniques of control – trapping people in artificially-created needs, and also simply indoctrinating them. Huge efforts go into that, and those are spiritual powers. They shouldn't be left out; they play a crucial role in the system of domination, and also in overcoming it.

Question: *Is there any possibility of struggle within the First World societies?*

Chomsky: Sure. In fact it's critical, because of their power. And the population faces somewhat similar problems. Inside the US and England, inequality has been growing very sharply. Real wages in the US (median real wages) have been declining since 1980. From 1980 until the last figures that are available, about ninety-five percent of families have lost real incomes. That's right through a period of considerable growth. Meanwhile, profits are shooting through the roof. Under those conditions, something like the structure of a Third World society is being created. Just as a small example, take the city where I live, Boston – a very wealthy city. It has a hospital that caters to the general population, Boston City Hospital, not for rich folks, but for everybody else. A couple of years ago they had to establish a clinic for malnutrition because for the first time they were getting cases of Third World-type malnutrition, mostly among children. They have to actually learn from Third World specialists how to deal with these things. They've been doing studies, and it turns out that there's a relationship between cold spells and malnutrition: a couple of weeks after a cold spell (Boston is very cold in the winter), the number of kids suffering from malnutrition increases. There are articles in medical journals about this. The reason is obvious: parents have to make an agonizing choice – do we heat our homes or do we feed our children? And you can't do both, because you're being forced down to Third World standards.

Well, under these conditions there are many prospects for struggle inside the First World societies, and I think this goes back to the question of spiritual powers. Many people are very upset and angry in the US, that's why the people in power often lose elections. People don't want the new guys, but they want to get rid of the guys in power. What emerges from this anger is a very complicated thing. In part it's very irrational, there's a proliferation of cults of every imaginable kind, religious fanaticism, paramilitary organizations, all kinds of social disorders. On the other hand, there are also signs of more constructive resistance, and which of those is going to win is a matter of what the earlier question called spiritual powers – what you come to understand and believe, what you are committed to and so on. Those are not predictable things; they are things to work on.

Question: *What is your view on the peace process in the Middle East?*

Chomsky: Actually, if I may say something unkind about India and other countries, this is not a bad example of spiritual powers. The term "peace process in the Middle East" is interesting in itself. In the US, the term "peace process" is used in a technical sense, to refer to whatever the US government has been doing. For instance, undermining peace, which it is often doing, is called "the peace process." Now, it's understandable that this terminology is used inside the US doctrinal system, but what is striking is that it's used everywhere.

Now take the Middle East, which is a fairly dramatic example. For twenty-five years, the US has been standing in the way of any peace process there. That began in 1971, when President Sadat of Egypt offered a full peace treaty to Israel in terms which were exactly the American official policy at the time. Israel didn't accept it, and the US had to make a choice – either go along with its ally or accept Egypt's offer and pursue its former policy. There was an internal debate over that – Henry Kissinger won, the US rejected Sadat's offer and instituted a policy that he called "stalemate," meaning no negotiations, no diplomacy, just violence. From that point till today, the US has stood virtually alone in the world in opposing every diplomatic initiative – that's called the peace process. The US vetoed Security Council resolutions, voted alone (with Israel, sometimes Dominica or some other client state) every year in the UN General Assembly and so on. Okay, finally the US position won. There are two basic points here. One is that the US was opposed to the withdrawal condition of UN 242, the basic document Washington had initiated in 1967 but rejected in 1971 (in practice, not formally). Secondly, it was opposed to Palestinian national rights. Palestinians don't have wealth or power; therefore they have no rights, that's elementary statecraft. Again, the US stood virtually alone in the world in opposing this. That's called the peace process – twenty-five years of activity to prevent any political settlement in the Middle East. And the US peace process finally won – the Oslo agreements simply ratify US rejectionism.

If you take a look at Oslo II, the interim agreement that has just been enacted and is being hailed as a great success (even in the Indian press, I noticed), what it does is to break up the West Bank into four regions. One of them is Greater Jerusalem, which is granted to Israel. If you take a look at the maps published in (say) the *New York Times* or in Israel, they just include that as a part of Israel. That's one zone. The second zone Israel just takes, period. That's seventy percent of the West Bank, totally under Israeli control. A third zone is granted to Palestinian authorities. That's two percent of the West Bank – mainly the municipal areas of various towns; Israel is delighted to give them up. The rest (the fourth zone) is called the region of autonomy. If you take a look at the map, it consists of about a hundred scattered regions inside the Israeli area of total control. In exchange for this magnanimous agreement, which is about as extreme as any proposal that has been made in the Israeli-US spectrum, the Palestinians have to accept the legality (present and future) of Israeli settlements and Israeli sovereign rights in state lands, absentee lands which could mean up to ninety percent of the autonomy territory. That's the settlement.

In fact, Israel is finally doing what is sensible. Instead of trying to run the Occupied Territories themselves, they want to run it the way the British ran India. The British didn't run India with the British army. They ran it with the Indian army: most of the troops that were controlling India were Indian troops, usually taken from one territory to beat up people of another territory. And that's the sensible mode of colonial control. In South Africa and Rhodesia, the same thing is true – the worst atrocities were carried out by the Black mercenaries. Central America is run the same way: the US army goes when needed, but mostly it is run by state security forces (basically terrorist forces, mercenaries like the British colonial army). And now Israel is finally doing the same thing – it's the only sensible way to run colonies. So the Palestinian mercenaries will control the population for them. They are pretty frank about it. Prime Minister Rabin, right after signing Oslo I, explained to the Israeli Parliament why there wouldn't be any security problems in Israel. Limited withdrawal was contemplated, he said, and when the Palestinian security forces come in and run the place there won't be any problems with appeals to the high court, or protests by human rights organizations or other bleeding hearts. These problems are going to end, because the mercenaries will be in charge. Well, that's standard imperial policy, certainly in India everybody ought to know it by heart. That's what they are instituting in those tiny areas they're going to withdraw from. Meanwhile, they keep the resources, most of the land, and so on.

This is a tremendous victory for power, and also a spiritual victory (to use that word again) because the world, amazingly, has accepted it. I discovered in interviews around the world, in Brazil, and western Europe, and so on, that people have forgotten what they believed themselves five years ago – namely they were advocating rights of self-determination for the Palestinians. Those rights have been lost, destroyed in the treaty, and that's called the peace process. That's a tremendous doctrinal victory – not just a victory for the rule of force on the ground but a victory of cultural hegemony, which is pretty impressive and it tells you something.

Question*: Do you have any comments on the World Bank, the IMF and the World Trade Organization in the context of structural adjustment programs for the Third World?*

Chomsky: Let me add to that, if I may, that the structural adjustment programs are also for the First World – with a somewhat different character, but rather similar in conception. On the World Bank, the IMF, the WTO and others like it, let me quote my favorite journal again, the *Financial Times* of London. A couple of years ago, it pointed out, I think accurately, that a "de facto world government" is taking form in "a new imperial age." That de facto world government is based on a few powerful states and an array of multinational corporations that rely on them and are closely linked to them and often to one another, and a set of transnational structures of governance including the IMF, the World Bank, the WTO, all operating pretty much without inspection – that's part of their beauty. I mean, theoretically you can figure out what's going on in the WTO, but for 99.9 percent of the population it's a total secret. This de facto world government is coalescing around the system of economic power. That's pretty much the way nation-states developed around national economies, and now it's happening around the global economy. It's a kind of quasi-governmental structure, immune from public accountability or even public awareness, serving the interests of global financial, industrial, service and other institutions. These global institutions are of course nationally rooted and rely heavily on state power – that they largely control – all that's quite important. They even have to be regularly bailed out by the national states, meaning the domestic population; otherwise many of them would collapse. So they are nationally rooted but global in character, and they need some kind of organizing structure around them. That's what this entire network is about, and why there are major attacks on democracy as well as markets.

   If you look at the Uruguay Round and other recent negotiations, you find a mixture of liberalization and protectionism, very carefully crafted to serve the needs of its primary constituents (mainly investors). The protectionist measures, as you know better than I do, are very much discussed in India, primarily because of the likely impact of the new intellectual property rights regime, a highly protectionist measure designed to destroy things like the Indian pharmaceutical industry, so that drug prices can shoot up, and so on and so forth. That's the way these things are crafted and they make perfect sense for that reason – they are serving the interests of the people who are designing them. These institutions have no legitimacy, and they are all fundamentally weak. They could be broken down by concerted popular action, but again that involves understanding what is going on and being willing to dedicate oneself to change it.

Question: *What are your comments on so-called economic liberalization in India?*

Chomsky: I don't feel competent to talk about the specific case of India. But we can see what happened in history and elsewhere. There are regular consequences of this so-called economic liberalization. For one thing, it's not liberalization. It's a mixture of liberalization and protection and subsidy, a kind of complicated transfer of resources and power. The effects are pretty marked. They often lead to reasonable macroeconomic statistics, so you get these economic miracles, but also to consistent decline in the social and economic health of a large majority of the population. And great success for a sector that's connected with international capital, and so on and so forth. Those are very consistent effects through Latin America and Africa, and I presume the same applies here in India.

Question: *With the end of the Cold War and the coming into being of a multipolar world, the US's self-proclaimed role is to continue to lead even through a decline in its economic competitiveness, which affects its ability to dictate global outcomes...*

Chomsky: I'm not sure what the question is, though the picture is certainly a common and understandable one. It's partly true, but partly misleading. For instance, when you talk of US economic decline you have to be rather cautious. Whether this is happening is a matter of definition. It depends on what you mean by the United States. If you mean the geographical area, yes there is an economic decline, for example the US share in world manufacturing has declined, there is a big trade deficit, and so on. On the other hand, if by US you mean the goods and services produced by US-based capital, then you get totally different results. If you look at US-based manufacturing corporations, their share in global production has not declined; in fact, it has probably increased. If you recalculate the US trade balance, as the Commerce Department recently did, by looking at exports of US corporations from overseas branches and affiliates as US exports, the US has a positive trade balance, not a trade deficit. From the point of view of the rulers, that's the way to do it. The *Wall Street Journal* has pointed that out. The people who are doing the bookkeeping for the transnationals do not care about the national border. They care about what their corporation is doing. If it's exporting from Brazil, that's as good as if it's exporting from Nevada, and the same is true globally. So, if by US you mean the people who run the show in the US, the US economy is not declining, in fact it may well be expanding its power. Similarly, the multipolar system appears in a different light if you look at the linkages across the big blocs, say Japan and the US and Europe. They are very closely interlinked at the level of real power, in all sorts of complicated ways, and those are the things that matter for people who run the show. If you think that through, you get a different picture; it's a complicated story, but I think that's the way to look at it.

Question: *Countries tend to favor the status quo as long as they perceive themselves as beneficiaries of it. They want change when they are on the other side. Even Indian criticism of the present discriminatory arrangement of the Security Council might change if India were made a permanent member. So it's basically a question of which side one is on.*

Chomsky: But I don't think one should talk of things like India as relevant entities in these matters. Here I think we should at least recognize what was obvious to, say, Adam Smith about two hundred years ago – that nations aren't entities. They are divided. As he put it, the "principal architects of policy" will make sure that their own interests are "most peculiarly attended to," whatever the impact on others. He was talking about England, where the principal architects of policy were the merchants and manufacturers. His point was that policy is made by the merchants and manufacturers, and they're making sure that they do fine, however grievous the impact on the people of England. That generalizes, and unless you accept those elementary truisms (ideas that later came to be called class analysis, but were trivialities two hundred years ago), you can't even talk realistically about the world. So for most of the people of India, does it matter if India is a member of the Security Council? What difference will it make? If they have a seat in the Security Council, then they'll do what the US tells them to do in the Security Council instead of somewhere else. To ninety percent of the people of India, it doesn't make any difference. Many probably won't even know about it. So, who cares? I mean, there are big problems in the UN, but they don't have anything much to do with who has a seat in the Security Council.

I really feel that people should think about the questions quite differently. The framework of the discussion is part of the technique of control of opinion, by which power remains stable. You should always ask yourselves, like you do in the sciences, whether the framework of discussion is acceptable. Most of the time, it's completely wrong; it's designed to confuse, and control, and marginalize. If you just think the problem through, it appears in a new light. So there are problems with the UN, but the question is not who are the permanent members in the Security Council. The obvious question to ask is why there should be any. Well, the system was designed to make sure that the superpowers at that time, and this primarily meant the US, would run the show completely. That's part of what is wrong about the UN. But changing the names of the placards isn't going to change that fact.

Question: *The leadership of the world has moved from the Netherlands to Britain to the US, and perhaps Japan next. One thing they share, one component of this global leadership since the industrial revolution, is the exploitation of nature through gross materialism (and thus development). How long can the earth survive that exploitation? Hasn't the time come for the historical struggle for existence to give way to cooperation and coexistence?*

Chomsky: Well, I don't really think that Japan is going to be the next big power center. We could discuss that. However, the general point certainly has something right about it, but that is only a concern for people, not for those who make decisions. If you are, say, running a business and you want to stay in this business, you can't be paying attention to whether the civilization is going to survive twenty years from now. You have to be paying attention to what the profits are going to be tomorrow, and if you don't pay attention to that, somebody else will eliminate you. That's the nature of a partially competitive system. There is some degree of competition in the system, and to the extent that competition exists, it drives people towards making short-term decisions which are quite irrational, in human terms. So these problems are definitely real. Global warming, for example, is not a joke. It could flood large parts of India, it's perfectly conceivable. Scientists don't know, they can just guess, but it could be really bad. But those things cannot be the concern of elements within the system that are seeking to maximize short-term gains. Therefore, they have to be the concern of someone else, and that concern can be implemented only in so far as unaccountable power is dissolved. If it remains in force, these problems will not be dealt with. And they are not trivial problems. If they are not dealt with in the near future, we may be faced with irreversible disaster.

Question: *How do you explain the Sino-US collaboration in the 1960s and 1970s?*

Chomsky: This is not a big problem. After gaining independence in the 1940s, China was interested in collaboration with the West. And the West would have accepted it on the same terms as Truman would have accepted collaboration with Russia, meaning we get our way eighty-five percent of the time, with China opened up to western penetration, investment and access to cheap labor and resources and so on. Within the US, there was a conflict in the 1950s, an important conflict about how to deal with China. You know the issue was a kind of hawk-dove conflict. Both groups had the same goal – to reintegrate China into the western-dominated world system. But the question was – do you do it better with a soft touch or a hard line? So should we be very hostile to China, drive it into an alliance with the Russians and smash them all up, or should we entice China into our system by trade and commerce or some other means? There are some good academic studies on this. It was a big issue in the 1950s. But by the 1960s the softer line was beginning to prevail. And incidentally, just to show how little the political labels mean, remember it was implemented by the hawks, namely Nixon and Kissinger. They're the ones who shifted policy towards incorporating China into the US system in the soft manner. And this happened to coincide well with things that were going on in China. So you get this collaboration. It was partly related to Great Power problems as well. The Sino-Soviet conflict was always real, real even back in the 1940s, and it had become quite severe by the early 1960s. So I don't see much problem in explaining that.

Question: *How do you envisage the trajectory of "socialism" now? Once the rotten apple gets power, may it not become as imperialistic and interventionist as the US is argued to be?*

Chomsky: Well, first of all I think that putting the word "socialism" in quotes is quite appropriate. The Soviet Union claimed to be "socialist" and "democratic." It was about as socialist as it was democratic. The West laughed properly at it being a "people's democracy," but it happily applauded the self-image of socialism because that's a good way to defame socialism. But both terms were equally accurate. The first thing that Lenin and Trotsky did when they took power in 1917 was to dismantle every socialist institution that had begun to develop spontaneously in the pre-revolutionary period. So factory councils, Soviets, everything was demolished. It was done on quite principled grounds. They were orthodox Marxists of a particular type; from their point of view, it didn't make sense for socialism to come to a pre-industrial society. The historical role of capitalism, according to this story, is to develop the industrial system in a cruel but efficient fashion. And then socialism comes along and makes it democratic and free and so on, so there's no place for socialism in Russia, a backward peasant society for which they had mostly contempt. They were carrying out a holding action, waiting for the revolution to take place in Germany – the advanced capitalist country where it was supposed to come about. There was an uprising, but it was crushed. They were left with power. Lenin at once turned to state capitalist methods (the new economic program), believing that socialism was just not possible, and nothing changed.

There was nothing socialist about the Soviet Union; in fact, it was one of the least socialist countries in the world, if socialism means what it always meant, namely at least workers' control over production. I mean, that's the beginning, and you had more of it in the West than you had in the Soviet Union, so there was no question of socialism. Naturally, it was a power system. It became imperialistic, like any other power system, so the prospects for socialism, I think, improved after the fall of the Soviet Union, just as they improved with the fall of fascism. A barrier to socialism had been removed, namely another system of autocracy and domination had been eliminated. Well, if you're a socialist surely you should celebrate that. Part of the victory of western doctrine has been to reinforce the belief, the crazy belief, that the system was socialist – so that people who are committed to socialist values are left kind of confused and disturbed and upset by the collapse of the Soviet Union, though in fact, it was one of the barriers to the achievement of socialism.

Question: *In this US-invented new world order, how much place does the Huntingtonian thesis of a "clash of civilizations" occupy?*

Chomsky: Well, with the collapse of the Cold War, a technique of doctrinal control collapsed. Until that point, any rotten thing that you did to the general population or abroad could be explained as an "unfortunate deviation from our traditional benevolence because of the Cold War." First of all, it's not the US. Let's go back to this notion of the "US-invented new world order." Actually, the phrase "new world order" appears over and over again – it appeared in 1990, actually twice in 1990, and here's another example of the influence of controlled opinion. In 1990, the term "new world order" was used for the first time in many years. It was used by the South Commission in their very important book, *The Challenge of the South* – that's the Commission that represents (more or less) the former non-aligned countries (something that India ought to know about given its history). The South Commission came out with an important volume, in which it called for a new world order based on global justice, and equity, and so on. Well, that one went over like a lead balloon. I wrote about it, and looked hard for something else, but could find virtually nothing. Who cares about studies produced by an organization devoted to interests and concerns of the vast majority of the world's population, but not its privileged and powerful sectors? A couple of months later, George Bush announced a "new world order," which he defined (to his credit) very simply: he said that in the new world order "what we say goes." That was while bombs were falling on Baghdad. So there are two versions of the new world order. It's not a US notion – it became a US notion because the voice of most of the population of the world never made it through the doctrinal barriers. I don't think the South Commission study, which was quite perceptive and interesting, was ever reviewed in the US. I don't know whether it was reviewed in India. But that was the first call for a new world order.

Okay, what about the Huntington thesis? First, the doctrinal system needs something new with the convenient Cold War pretexts gone. In fact, right through the 1980s, when it was pretty obvious that the Russians weren't going to be around for too long, there was an increasingly desperate search for some alterative technique of controlling the population. So if you look through the 1980s, the threat was changing. It was international terrorism, or crazed Arabs, or Hispanic narco-traffickers, or one thing or another. Huntington is a big thinker, the Professor of "the Science of Government" at Harvard. He came along with *Clash of Civilizations*. It has a sort of nice ring to it, though it didn't mean anything, though with some effort it could be created. There is no more of a clash of civilizations today than there ever was. He's talking about an alleged conflict between the US (between the western civilization) and Islam, but if you look at the connections, they cross all over the place. One of the leading US allies is the most extreme Islamic fundamentalist state in the world, namely Saudi Arabia. As long as the rulers of Saudi Arabia understand what their duty is, namely to ensure that the profits from oil production go to the West, they can be whatever they like – Islamic fundamentalists or whatever they please. The most populous Islamic state is Indonesia, which has been a close friend and ally ever since Suharto came to power with a huge mass slaughter of mostly landless peasants, also destroying the mass-based political party that represented their interests, and turned the country into a "paradise for investors." The Reaganites gathered the most extreme radical fundamentalists they could find anywhere in the world, brought them to Afghanistan, armed and trained them – not to defend Afghanistan, which could have been legitimate, but to harm the Russians. They left Afghanistan to their tender mercies, once the task was over. Meanwhile, the Reaganites supported Zia ul-Haq as he brought extreme Islamic fundamentalism to Pakistan. They even pretended they didn't know he was building nuclear weapons.

Let's continue with the 1980s. Well, the great enemy of the US in Central America was the Catholic Church. Large segments of the Catholic Church in Latin America had undertaken what they called the "preferential option for the poor." They were organizing peasants and helping them to set up base communities and peasant associations. That is impermissible: it might lead to democracy and desperately needed social reform in these horror chambers. Accordingly, it set off a massive campaign of state terrorism effectively based in Washington. The decade opened with the murder of an Archbishop by elements closely aligned with the US, and ended with the murder of six leading Jesuit intellectuals by an elite battalion armed and trained by the US. And in between, you had very much the same story. So, was that a clash of civilizations? The US versus Catholicism? No, it was the usual clash, in fact the old North-South clash. Here was a part of the service areas which was trying to seek an independent role – that's not allowed. They can be Catholic, or Islamic, or secular democrats, whatever you want. It's the independence and particularly the danger of successful development on an independent path – that's just not acceptable. So I don't see any reason to believe in any clash of civilizations. There is just the old clash that always has to be disguised. It has to be disguised, because however well you understand it internally, the general public isn't supposed to understand it. In fact, Huntington himself has been very clear about that. He's pointed out frankly and honestly that during the whole Cold War period, US military intervention abroad often had to be justified by pretending that there was a conflict with the Russians, to mask it from the general population. He said that – in approximately those words – and it's accurate. And he understands that well enough to understand it in the case of the new clash of civilizations.

Question: *If power rules the roost and it's too bad (the leading examples are the USA and the USSR), then are you welcoming Hitler? If not, what is your alternative?*

Chomsky: That's an interesting array of alternatives. The question is which gangster should order us around? There is another alternative – no gangster orders us around. We'll get rid of all of them, and try to move towards democracy. That's the alternative that I would suggest. It's a pretty obvious one – there is nothing profound about it. And it is within reach.

2. The Vicissitudes of Democracy: Part 1*

The current period, as you know, is commonly described as a period of unprecedented flourishing of democracy and markets. Let me begin by clarifying my own point of view on this general topic. In my view, the most striking feature of the current period is not the flourishing of democracy and markets, but a major attack on democracy, human rights and even markets. One aspect of this is a kind of experiment, an unprecedented experiment, to extend to the rich industrial societies (primarily the US, England, the Anglo-American societies) something like the structural model of the Third World. By this, I mean societies that are sharply stratified into a small sector of extreme wealth and power, a huge mass of people who are living somewhere between unpleasantness and utter misery, and another group of people who are simply superfluous for profit-making, and therefore have no rights, and have to be disposed of in some fashion or other. You can't take a walk in an American city or most British ones without recognizing the Third World. Things look somewhat different, because these cities are obviously much richer. But the structure is there, and is being imposed by conscious social policy. It has nothing to do with the laws of nature, or the market and its infinite wisdom, or various things to which this is attributed. It is perfectly deliberate social policy, making use of institutional possibilities that have existed for some years, and are being used for this purpose. Well, I want to fill in some of the pieces of that point of view – but let me begin with the concept of democracy, which I think is at the heart of the whole matter.

---

* Lecture delivered at the Delhi School of Economics on 12 January 1996.

http://dx.doi.org/10.11647/OBP.0050.02

Democracy, like many other terms of political discourse, has become so abused in recent years as to be virtually useless. Recall, for instance, the "people's democracies" of eastern Europe. Recognizing the absurdity of that use of the term democracy, one might be surprised by a recent article by one of the outstanding students of contemporary American democracy, Robert McChesney (professor at the University of Wisconsin), who writes that in the second half of the twentieth century, only the former USSR, among the industrial countries, approached the US for its level of mass depoliticization. He says it's one of the reigning paradoxes in social theory, since the US has perhaps the most solidly established democratic institutions of any country and is sometimes even described as "an inspiration for the triumph of democracy in our time" (I'm quoting the editors of *The New Republic*, at what's considered the liberal end of the mainstream spectrum). Well, the vast majority of the American population disagrees with the standard elite perception and accepts the rather dim view that McChesney describes. So eighty percent of the population in the US believe that the government, in the wording of the polls, works for the few and the special interests, not for the people. This proportion has sharply increased, from a fairly steady fifty percent that have given that answer for some years now; similarly, over eighty percent regard the economic system as inherently unfair (in the wording of the polls), and half the population thinks that both the political parties should be disbanded. Voting is low; it has been declining through the years.

The same is true of participation in the kinds of secondary organizations that are the foundation of any functioning democracy. That's part of a more general and striking phenomenon that Harvard political scientist Robert Putnam has called the strange disappearance of civic America. In the past thirty years of increasing cynicism and alienation, people's participation in any form of social activity has declined by about half. That's a substantial fall, and it includes everything, from participation in various political and social groups to parent-teacher associations, listening to talks, even joining bowling leagues – it's fallen very radically. There are, in fact, counter-trends, very clear and significant, but they are not studied much because they have a dissident character, so they're outside the domain of inquiry for a respectable study. Nevertheless, the general phenomenon is quite real, and it is true to say, as Putnam does, that civil society has pretty much collapsed – a dramatic and striking fact. The mass depoliticization that McChesney is talking about is part of that.

Quite generally, public attitudes differ substantially from the way they are portrayed. In 1984, for example, Ronald Reagan won a landslide victory, which was called a popular mandate for conservatives. And indeed, he was chosen as a "real conservative" by a section of the voters, actually four percent of the voters, which means that two percent of the electorate chose him because he was a real conservative. That's what is called a landslide victory for conservatives in contemporary rhetoric. About sixty percent of voters hoped that his legislative programs would *not* be enacted. In general, Reagan's popularity was mostly a media fabrication – it was nothing special, and by 1992 he was ranking right with Nixon as the most unpopular living ex-President. Public opinion studies, right through the so-called period of conservatism, showed a steady drift towards vaguely New Deal style – roughly "social democratic welfare state" – liberalism, even willingness to accept higher taxes if they are used for public social spending (for health, education, environmental protection, helping the poor, and so on). The major priority of the population, steadily in the polls, is for stimulative activities on the part of the government to create decent employment – that has been the highest priority and remains so. All these attitudes persist without substantial change. However, these concerns and attitudes of the general population are simply not articulated in the political arena. The divorce has always been significant, and by now, it's dramatic. That's one reason why voting has been so limited and declining, and also why it's so skewed toward the wealthy (the richer you are, the more likely you are to vote). Another aspect of this is that political campaigns are pretty much a form of marketing, which nobody takes seriously, except the political commentators, newspapers, and intellectuals, who are paid to take it seriously – the population doesn't.

These factors were very dramatic in the latest election (November 1994). Quite regularly, campaign spending is a pretty good predictor of electoral victory. In 1994, you could predict who was going to win with ninety percent accuracy if you simply asked who spent more than his or her opponent. The voting was skewed toward the wealthy, even more than usual. That probably accounts for most of the shift in votes from 1992 when Clinton won. This 1994 election is called a conservative landslide – in fact, the percentage shift was about two percent. About twenty percent of the electorate, which means a bare majority of participants (participants are a little over a third of the population), voted for the Republicans. One out of six voters considered the election to be an affirmation of the Republican agenda. Only a quarter of the population had ever heard of the famous "Contract with America," the Republican agenda. This was actually a PR stunt, cooked up at the last minute, and a large majority of the population opposed its individual provisions when they were asked about them. The leader of this "political earthquake," as it is called, Newt Gingrich, was quite unpopular at the time, and his rankings have dropped very severely since. He is now one of the most unpopular figures in American politics.

The people who chose to participate in the 1994 elections were mostly voting the rascals out, and that's the way it usually is. People don't really care what their stand is, just get rid of them. Anybody can do better. There were a few candidates, not many, who tried to mobilize the traditional popular Democratic coalition (labor, minorities, the poor, etc.). They actually did quite well in the 1994 elections. The ones who got smashed were the Clinton New Democrats, whom the population regards, rightly, as less extreme Republicans – they lost very badly. If you take a look at non-voters, which is a majority of the population, their opinion profiles match very closely with those of voters who voted Democratic. But there's just very little participation on the part of people who would support a populist left coalition committed to equitable economic growth and political democracy, *if* such an opinion were allowed to intrude into the political arena, which it is not. In its absence, many people are turning to religious fanaticism, which is quite extraordinary in the US, probably the most fundamentalist country in the world, more than Iran, I assume. Cults of every imaginable kind, including paramilitary organizations, all sorts of irrationality are flourishing. These are pretty ominous developments, they have precedents, which we remember without much pleasure, and, by now, these developments are beginning to concern even corporate executives, who otherwise approve very highly of the actions of the Gingrich army and their dedication to the rich and privileged.

The new Congress, claiming this popular mandate, moved very quickly to dismantle sixty years of social spending. This is a dramatic illustration of the paradox of mass depoliticization within well-established institutions of formal democracy. In general, government policy and public attitudes are quite at variance, but, as I said, the discrepancy in the last few years has been really startling. When this conservative mandate was allegedly granted last November, about sixty percent of the population wanted an *increase* in social spending. Large majorities are in favor of high social spending for health, education, environmental protection, and so on.

There is hardly a single issue on which policy even resembles public opinion. A striking example relates to balancing the budget. That's the central issue in Washington; as you probably know, the government's been closed down for a couple of months. It's the highest priority for both political parties – they agree about balancing the budget and differ only on the time frame, say, whether it should be seven years or seven and a half years. The numbers change around a little bit, and so on. If you listen to the US press or radio, you hear endlessly that Americans voted for a balanced budget – that is false. Or, let's be more precise – half false. The US is a very heavily polled society. Business wants to keep its finger on the public pulse. But polls have to be read very carefully. In their design, there's usually one set of questions for headline writers, and another set of questions for people who want to know how to design propaganda properly. They want to know what the people are thinking; and the budget is a good case. There is a question that says, "Would you like to have the budget balanced?" and everybody says, "sure." It's like saying, would you like your debts magically eliminated? Then comes the next question, which is the serious question: would you like to have your debts eliminated if it means you lose your house, car, and refrigerator, and your children can't go to school? And everybody says, "no." It's the same with that question here. If people are asked, "Do you want the budget balanced under any realistic conditions?" – an overwhelming majority oppose it. But that, as I said, is for people who want to know how to package and market things. The first question, do you want the budget balanced, is for the headline writers, and they aren't lying when they say that people want their debts magically eliminated. In fact, what the population continues to want are stimulative programs for job growth, the growth of decent jobs. The standard welfare package remains very popular.

Now, there remains a section of the population that thinks that balancing the budget is the highest priority. It's five percent. That's the same as the proportion that think that homelessness is the highest priority. However, that five percent happens to include the people who count in the political system, namely the corporate and financial community. So if you read the business press, say *BusinessWeek*, there's a headline saying that "American business has spoken, Balance the budget." That's based on a poll of business executives, and when business speaks, the political class listens, the intellectuals say what they're supposed to say, and the press tells you that's the story, which it is – for the people who matter.

Why does business want the budget balanced? As an economic policy, it really does not make a lot of sense. Aside from conforming to very narrow short-term profit interests, budget balancing is mainly a weapon that can be used against social programs. These have been declining quite severely for some years. There was something called a war on poverty, which is supposed to have failed, but what's not usually mentioned is that the war was barely even a skirmish that lasted about two to three years, and it ended with Nixon, who was the last liberal President. By the early 1970s, welfare programs were declining very sharply, and with quite harmful effects. Part of the Third World character of much of urban society is the result of that. Of the current debt, about eighty percent comes from the Reagan years. The Reagan administration succeeded, within a few years, in turning the nation from the world's leading creditor nation into the world's leading debtor, and that was quite consciously intended as a weapon against social spending. The weapon can now be used to ensure that government programs are focused even more narrowly on the welfare of the people who count – the rich and the privileged, who have a huge welfare state which not only remains, but is increasing without any concern for balancing the budget. I'll return to those steps. But they should, they're intended to, and doubtless will, increase the huge profits of the past years. The business press is utterly euphoric about the prospects and describes them as dazzling, stupendous, and so on.

The US has been a business-run society pretty much from its origins, and the scale is impressive. Every year, *Fortune*, the leading business monthly, publishes a list called Fortune 500 – the 500 biggest corporations. This year, the Fortune 500 controlled two-thirds of the GDP, as well as a very substantial portion of the international economy, and that's why we know so much about public attitudes. These guys who run the place want to know what the public is thinking. One of their major activities, in fact, is marketing. About a trillion dollars a year are spent simply on marketing – that's one-seventh of GDP. Its practitioners understand very well (and they are kind enough to tell us, if we read their publications to one another) that marketing is mainly a matter of manipulation and control. That doesn't mean only creating artificial wants and making people buy goods they don't need or want; it also involves marketing ideas and attitudes. The PR industry is a huge industry. Its leading figure was Edward Bernays, who was incidentally a good Wilson-Roosevelt-Kennedy liberal. In the 1920s, he described the "engineering of consent" as the "very essence of the democratic process," "the freedom to persuade and to suggest." Now, of course, as you recognize, freedom happens to be concentrated in a few hands. But that's just the notion of free society that we all have drilled into us from childhood. There are many illustrations of this. One of the most striking is the history of the electronic media in the United States. The US is unusual, perhaps unique, in that radio was very quickly handed over to private corporations with scarcely any gesture toward public interest. It was interesting to watch the discussion about it. Even progressives or so-called civil libertarians regarded this giveaway of radio to private power as a victory for democracy – as power to the people, namely RCA, GE, and so on. The same was true about TV without even any discussion. Just a couple of weeks ago, the internet, which, of course, was publicly created, was handed over to private power as well. What about the print media? They aren't controlled by private power, rather, they *are* huge corporations, parts of bigger conglomerates – they are in business, like everything else. They sell a product – the product is audiences, which they sell to other businesses, called advertisers. The elite press, which sets the agenda for most of the rest, like the *New York Times* and the *Washington Post*, is made up of big corporations which sell privileged audiences to other businesses. And, not surprisingly, the picture of the world that emerges from this interaction reflects the interests of the sellers, the buyers and the product. It would be pretty amazing if it didn't. This non-surprising fact has been documented beyond serious dispute, and the effects are often pretty remarkable.

It also comes as no big surprise that "politics is the shadow cast on society by big business" – I'm quoting America's leading twentieth- century social philosopher John Dewey, who added quite realistically that "attenuation of the shadow will not change the substance." And in its own way, the public grasps this, as the facts mentioned earlier indicate; although with mass depoliticization, the collapse of civil society, and narrowly constrained doctrinal institutions, public perceptions are often very confused and quite irrational. On the other hand, the business world has tight organization, ample resources, and a high level of class consciousness. They see themselves as fighting a bitter class war, and have done so for a long time. Business has long understood that what it calls the "public mind" is "the only serious danger confronting the company," AT&T in this case, but the AT&T corporate executive, quoted early in the century, is expressing a much more general view, among those whom Adam Smith called "the masters of mankind." The people who spend trillions of dollars a year in marketing ideas, as well as goods, have long understood the lesson expressed by Bernays, who wrote an influential manual for the rising PR industry in 1928, in which he explained that "the conscious and intelligent manipulation of the organized habits and opinions of the masses is an important element in democratic society... It is the intelligent minorities which need to make use of propaganda continuously and systematically." The intelligent minorities aren't intelligent because they have high IQs or anything like that, but because they have the good sense to serve the proper masters – that's the criterion of intelligence, and, of course, it's not a special feature of the US. The term propaganda was used quite openly in those more frank days. Today, after the Nazis and the Second World War, people don't like the word, so they call it something else. Back in the 1920s and 1930s, it was straightforwardly called "propaganda," which it is.

To control the public mind, you need to know what people are thinking, and what their attitudes are. This is the reason for the heavy polling – it's a side benefit for the people who want to know the truth, because we can look at the business journals where the polls are, and find out what people are thinking. So take, say, this "Contract with America," which is run through Congress, and it's going to have a big effect on American life. It's constantly described as poll-driven; they say Washington is simply responding to public will in a pluralist democracy. Here we have another paradox – polls show clearly that the public overwhelmingly opposes the policies that are enacted under public pressure. Social spending has been cut, when people want it to go up, and military spending is going up, when people are opposed to that by six to one – that's the last thing that people want raised in all the polls.

How can the Republican agenda then be called poll-driven? That's not false, and the answer was given by the polling specialist of the Gingrich Republicans, Frank Luntz, and reported in the business press under the headline "GOP pollsters never measure popularity of 'Contract', only slogans." Luntz told reporters that a majority of Americans supported each of the ten parts of the Contract. What he meant, he conceded, is that a majority liked the slogans that were being used to package it. So the public opposes slashing the health system, but it favors "protecting the health system." Slashing the health system is called "protecting the health system," and it turns out that people favor that, and so on, down the line.

All this is quite natural in a society dominated by institutions of private power, which are devoted to undermining the threat of democracy for perfectly good reasons. That's the resolution of the apparent paradox of mass depoliticization within democratic institutions. In fact, it's the resolution that's pointed out in the article I mentioned earlier. McChesney was reviewing an important book by an old friend of mine who died recently, an Australian social scientist named Alex Carey. The book is called *Taking the Risk Out of Democracy*. Carey pioneered the study of corporate propaganda, and his book is a collection of essays, which are largely unknown, just as the topic itself is rarely studied. Actually, the first academic study of corporate propaganda appeared in the US just a few months ago, which is a very remarkable fact. There is no doubt that corporate propaganda is a leading feature of modern society and culture, but it is almost never studied, and the reason is clear enough. The shadow that's cast over the political system by private power extends to every other part of the social order as well. The last thing that those who cast it want is for people to understand what they're up to, and that's understood in the political science community as well. So there's a position at Harvard, one of my favorite titles, called the Professorship of the Science of Government, which is held by Samuel Huntington, a good source of quotes, who wrote an important book called *American Politics*, in which he pointed out that "the architects of power in the United States must create a force that can be felt, but not seen. Power remains strong when it remains in the dark. Exposed to the sunlight, it begins to evaporate." This is a useful message, but for the general public, different mantras are preferred.

Alex Carey opens his most important essay by formulating and at once resolving the paradox of depoliticization under democracy, and he puts it succinctly and correctly. Carey writes that "the twentieth century has been characterized by three developments of great political importance: the growth of democracy; the growth of corporate power; and the growth of corporate propaganda as a means of protecting corporate power against democracy." And that conclusion extends very broadly, it extends to much of what reaches the general public through the media and the journals of opinion, and, in fact, it extends to a good deal more of scholarship than its practitioners like to admit. Individual attitudes remain resilient, as the polls I mentioned earlier indicate, and remarkably so, given the fact that they receive no support. People don't hear them; people just feel them, and they're held in isolation, but nevertheless, that propaganda offensive has taken its toll. The striking fanaticism in the country (cults, religious fanaticism and that sort of thing) is one effect of the success of corporate propaganda, as is the collapse of civil society. The people who would have been working, say, sixty years ago, to build industrial unions are now joining paramilitary organizations. Look at the people who are accused of blowing up the federal building, take a look at their social profiles, class backgrounds, and so on. They're much the same people who would've been working to create the CIO sixty years ago. They are angry, and that's understandable (their lives have fallen apart), but they are also very confused. So over eighty percent of the population thinks that working people don't have influence on what goes on, but only twenty percent think that unions don't have enough influence. In fact, about forty percent consider them *too* influential – workers don't have enough influence, but unions have too much influence. That's the general view.

Take NAFTA, the seriously mislabeled North American Free Trade Agreement (the only thing that's true about that description is that it had to do with North America). NAFTA was strongly opposed by the general public, despite a huge propaganda barrage. However, the same people who opposed NAFTA condemned the unions that were lobbying for, very much, the positions that they held. Although of course, they really couldn't know that, because the positions of the labor movement were simply excluded from the media, in pretty remarkable ways.

Take foreign aid. It's supposed to be very unpopular, and, on the surface, it does look very unpopular. However, when you look a little more closely, you discover several things. Firstly, people vastly overestimate how much foreign aid the US gives, and when they're asked how much they think the US should give, they say more than it actually is. People are even willing to accept higher taxes if there is foreign aid that goes to the poor. They correctly understand that it doesn't, even if they don't know the details. They do oppose foreign aid, but they want it to be higher than it is. And certainly, they don't know that the US foreign aid program is the most miserly in the developed world. It virtually disappears if you eliminate the biggest component, which happens to go to a rich society. Very few people know that foreign aid is basically a form of export promotion. In most countries, foreign aid is aid from the taxpayer to domestic-based corporations that happens to pass through some other country, which may incidentally benefit from it or may not.

The same is true of welfare at home. People vastly overestimate its scale. They think that the government has the responsibility to help the poor, but they want welfare cut back – very similar to the attitude towards unions. And, of course, very few people are aware that the Pentagon system is primarily a welfare system for the rich. What has happened? What has happened is that people are inundated with propaganda (including movies, TV, newspapers) that depicts unions as enemies of the worker, black mothers on welfare breeding like rabbits and driving Cadillacs, liberal elites and petty bureaucrats stealing money and interfering in our lives, and the whole familiar refrain. All of that has left attitudes pretty much unchanged, but it has left people very confused.

The current mood is conventionally and accurately described as the mood of anti-politics. That says – get the rascals out, get rid of the government. Intensive propaganda has succeeded in erasing from people's minds an understanding of the most elementary aspect of contemporary reality, namely that politics may be bad but the reason is that it's the shadow cast by business over society. And naturally, you're not supposed to see what casts the shadow, only the shadow. That's what the propaganda focuses on, and it makes good sense for those who cast the shadow to focus people's attention on the government. Propaganda focuses on the evils of the government, because one of the good things about government is that, at least in principle, and sometimes even in fact, it can be influenced by the general public. That's not true of the private tyrannies (basically, totalitarian institutions) that cast the shadow. They can't be influenced even in principle. So, to the extent that power can be shifted to them, the threat of democracy is reduced.

This has been going on for a long time. After the First World War, Woodrow Wilson carried out a Red Scare, which was quite something. It decimated the labor movement and pretty much eliminated independent thought. At that point, the business world, and the self-designated "intelligent minorities" who serve its interests, thought that the game was over, that we've reached the end of history. Well, a couple of years later, there was an unexpected and substantial popular mobilization, which demonstrated that the euphoria over the end of history was wrong – not the first time, and not the last. Business reacted to this with considerable alarm. In the mid-1930s, when the US was kind of being brought into the industrial world with standard welfare programs, business publications warned of what they called "the hazards facing the industrialists in the newly realized political power of the masses." Incidentally, the tone of this should not surprise you. Business publications read like vulgar Marxist tracts, with the values reversed but the same kind of terminology. Words like "the masses" can't be used in general discourse today, except by business. So they were worried about the newly realized power of the masses: "we are definitely heading for adversity" unless their thinking is directed to more proper channels. This is the National Association of Manufacturers (NAM); its PR budget increased by a factor of twenty between 1934 and 1937, right at the time when the New Deal measures were being passed. And that hazard only grew in severity with the Second World War, as the US population joined the social democratic currents that were sweeping the better part of the world, and the business world knew it. One leading PR firm warned, in 1947, that our present economic system and the men who run it had three years, maybe five at the outside, to resell our preferred way of life as against competing systems. The chairman of the PR advisory committee for the NAM called for a huge campaign to win "the everlasting battle for the minds of men" and to "stem the current drift towards socialism." The NAM distributed 18 million pamphlets from 1946 to 1950, about forty percent of them to the workforce, as part of what the business press described as an extensive program to indoctrinate employees. The rest mostly went to students, community leaders, and business leaders. Business propaganda was reaching about 70 million people, *Fortune* editor Daniel Bell wrote at the time, along with other propaganda that he called "staggering" and prodigious in its scale: by the early 1950s, about 20 million people a week were reported to be watching business-sponsored films. Another PR executive explained that the entertainment industry was enlisted for the cause, portraying unions as the enemy, the outsider disrupting the harmony of the American way of life, and otherwise helping to indoctrinate the citizens with the capitalist story. In fact, every aspect of social life was targeted – schools, universities, churches, even recreational programs. To indicate the scale, by 1954, one third of the material that students were using in public schools was designed and funded by business. At that time there still was a labor press, and it sought to combat what it called the plan "to sell the American people on the virtues of big business." They recognized that the commercial media world would follow the policy of "damning labor at every opportunity, while carefully glossing over the sins of the banking and industrial magnates who really control the nation." Those are quotes from some of the 800 labor papers which, at that time, still reached about 20-30 million people, and had survived for about a hundred years. A hundred years earlier, they were more or less on the scale of the capitalist press. In the 1950s they were seeking, in their own words, to expose racial hatred and "all kinds of anti-democratic words and deeds," and to provide "antidotes for the worst poisons of the kept press." But, of course, working people entirely lacked the resources to compete, and this independent press disappeared shortly afterwards, and is forgotten from memory.

The story continues to the present, including the "concerted efforts" of corporate America "to change the attitudes and values of workers" and convert "worker apathy into corporate allegiance," and Advertising Council campaigns "saturating the media and reaching practically everybody," as the business press describes the campaigns. "Chairs of Free Enterprise" and other measures have been initiated to subvert the educational system. There is no time to review here the impressive array of measures that have been deployed by a highly class-conscious business community, which has always seen itself as fighting a bitter class war, and for whom cost is no consideration. So effectively has functioning civil society been dismantled that Congress can now ram through programs opposed by large majorities, who are left in fear, anger, and hopelessness.

The achievement is real. Yale University labor historian David Montgomery has pointed out that, "For working people, the most important part of the Jeffersonian legacy was the shelter it provided to free association, diversity of beliefs and behavior, and defiance of alleged social superiors in society." The structures of civil society "obstructed bourgeois control of American life at every turn." That is the basic motivation for the unremitting campaigns to demolish the independent press and effective forms of community solidarity, from trade unions to political clubs and organizations. They have been conducted with passionate intensity and considerable success.

The history of the labor movement is probably the most important part of the story in the US. As you know, society's working class organizations have traditionally been the main mechanism by which ordinary people have been able to pool their very limited resources and act in their own common interests, which is the interest of the large majority – that's been a major factor in the extension of democracy and human rights. US labor history is interesting. For one thing, it is very violent, more so than in other industrial societies. It was not until the Great Depression in the 1930s that elementary rights were won, and they have been steadily eroded in the postwar years, very dramatically in the Reagan years. The Reaganites openly fostered corporate crime, outright corporate crime, to destroy the remnants of the industrial union years, as the business press, incidentally, has recorded rather accurately. This idea of democracy as a threat is not obscure. In the public domain, more exalted rhetoric is preferred, but for the "intelligent minority" the idea is commonplace. So at the time when Bernays was teaching the business world about the need to manipulate the organized habits and opinions of the masses, one of the leading public intellectuals, Walter Lippmann, was writing his influential "Progressive Essays on Democracy," in which he describes the new modes of "manufacture of consent" as a revolution in the practice of democracy. Like Bernays, Lippmann had served in the first government propaganda organization, established by Woodrow Wilson to try to turn a mostly pacifist population into jingoist fanatics and warmongers, a purpose in which it was extremely successful. That feat impressed Lippmann, as it impressed Bernays, and also others, among them Hitler, who writes about it quite bitterly. Hitler felt that Germany was never able to combat the powerful and effective Anglo-American propaganda systems, and he vowed that, next time around, Germany would be ready to compete. Going back to Lippmann, he develops a theory of democracy. The public, he says, are "ignorant and meddlesome outsiders" who must not be allowed to intrude in the management of public affairs. They do have what he calls a "function" in a democracy, namely "spectators" but not "participants." They are permitted to select, now and then, among responsible men. That point was elaborated by one of the founders of modern political science, leading liberal thinker Harold Lasswell. He has an entry on "propaganda" in the *Encyclopedia of Social Sciences* (this is pre-war, they still used the word), where he warns that we should not "succumb to democratic dogmatisms about men being the best judges of their own interests" – they're not. They must be reduced to mass depoliticization for their own good.

These are very conventional ideas and they continue more recently. In the 1970s, for instance, the first study of the Trilateral Commission was devoted to what it called the "crisis of democracy" in the US, Europe, and Japan (the trilateral regions). The crisis was very frankly explained. In the 1960s, large sections of the population that are usually passive and apathetic began to organize and articulate their interests, and tried to get them into the public arena and press for them. Well, if you're naive, you might think that's democracy. If you are the intelligent minority, you understand that this is a crisis of democracy that has to be overcome. People have to be restored to passivity and obedience in the name of democracy. Therefore, the Commission suggested mass depoliticization, perhaps even a return to the good old days when "Truman had been able to run the country with the cooperation of a relatively small number of Wall Street lawyers and bankers," so we had real democracy. That was a quote from the Professor of Science of Government at Harvard. Maybe such nostalgia involves a little bit of exaggeration, but he got the point right.

All the opinions that I've been sampling so far are from the democratic end of the spectrum, the liberal end, in the American sense of the word "liberal." At the other extreme, you get reactionary ideas of the Reagan-Gingrich variety (mislabeled "conservative"). They don't agree that the "ignorant and meddlesome outsiders" should even be spectators. That is why they have such a fascination with secrecy, deceit, clandestine operations and other methods to undermine the functioning of democracy. Take, say, clandestine operations. The extent to which a country is involved in clandestine operations is usually a pretty good measure of elite hatred of democracy, because clandestine operations aren't secret from everybody. They are certainly not secret from the victims. They know all about it. Take for example the huge clandestine operations that the Reagan administration was running in Central America in the 1980s. Obviously, the people of Central America knew all about it, people were getting slaughtered. They were well known to the big international terrorist network that the US set up. Remember that the US is a big player. It's not like Libya. Libya may hire individual terrorists, but the US hires terrorist states. That's what you do when you're a big guy, so that the terrorist network included Taiwan, Israel, England, Saudi Arabia – big terrorist states. They all knew about it. In fact, the truth of the matter is that the clandestine operations were even known to the press, but they were sort of behind enough clouds, so that you could pretend shock and dismay over this terrible thing when something leaked out. Well, that's what these clandestine operations are all about. They're mostly to keep the domestic population in ignorance, out of an understanding that the population is not going to be pleased if they know about it. And the Reaganites went to extremes in this, as in other methods of undermining democracy, because they don't believe that the public ought to be spectators.

There have been a lot of changes since (say) the days of David Ricardo, but few in the mainstream disagree with Ricardo's principle that the franchise is okay as long as it is limited, in his words, "to that part of [the people] which cannot be supposed to have any interest in overturning the right of property." And you need heavier restrictions, he said, if "limiting the elective franchise to the very narrowest bounds" would guarantee more "security for a good choice of representatives," who have a proper understanding of the rights of property – the main right. The fact that unaccountable private power would undermine democracy is not new either, that was well understood by classical liberal opinion. Thomas Jefferson, for example, warned in his later years that the rising "banking institutions and moneyed incorporations" would destroy the freedom won in the American Revolution. They would become the "single and splendid government of an aristocracy, founded on banking institutions, and moneyed incorporations," which would enable the few to be "riding and ruling over the plundered ploughman and beggared yeomanry," destroying democracy and restoring a form of absolutism if given a free hand, as indeed they were, to a degree that exceeded Jefferson's worst nightmares, although not through the expression of popular will. Those corporations achieved their extraordinary power primarily through courts and lawyers, acting in what we might call "technocratic insulation" from the general public, to borrow some World Bank lingo. That's what is supposed to happen: in the end the governments are supposed to act in technocratic insulation, so that the public doesn't know what's going on and can't get in the way. A few years after Jefferson, Alexis de Tocqueville, in his famous writings on democracy in America, expressed his concern that "the manufacturing aristocracy, which is growing up under our eyes," and which "is one of the harshest that has ever existed in the world," might escape its confines, spelling the end of democracy. Like Jefferson and other classical liberals, Adam Smith and de Tocqueville understood equality of condition, not equality of opportunity, to be the necessary condition for democracy, and valued it in its own right. That's standard classical liberalism, and if you look back at the much misunderstood Adam Smith, he framed his rather nuanced arguments for markets on the assumption that, under conditions of perfect liberty, markets would tend towards perfect equality. That's the moral justification for them, whatever you think of the argument.

It should also be recalled that Jefferson and his radical democratic ideals were very far from the thinking of the founders of American democracy, and they left very little impact on political thinking since, although they had considerable impact on popular culture. The present fragmentation and isolation, which is such a striking feature of American society, should actually be understood as a realization of the ideals on the basis of which the country was founded – the ideals of the founding fathers. Before saying something about that, it's worth bearing in mind that the US (which is really the paradigm example of modern democracy, the most important one to look at, aside from its power) is about as close to a *tabula rasa* as anything this complicated world permits. It was an invented society. The native population was eliminated, removed, and a New World was constructed, with very little residue from traditional institutions and structures. That's one of the reasons, I think, for the big difference between the US and other parts of the industrial world. It's also the reason for the lack of an authentic conservative tradition in the US – there isn't any because the conservative institutions never existed. What's called conservatism is actually reactionary statism. I think it's also probably the reason for the relatively weak social support system. If you look at how these actually developed in other parts of the industrial world, to a significant extent they developed out of very reactionary traditional social forms that had a pre-capitalist ideology. Remember, before the great innovations of Ricardo, Malthus, and classical economists (what's now called neo-liberal economics), before that period, people had the odd idea that humans have a right to live. In feudal society, people had a place, maybe a lousy place, but some sort of a place and the right to live in that place. Ricardo, Malthus, Nassau Senior and others thought that was a mistake – they had no right to life. The only right they have is what they can gain in the market. And if you can't survive by those means, then you must go somewhere else – and in those days, that meant going to America and killing the natives, or to Australia and doing the same, and so on. And now there is the same message, but nowhere else to go. The principle is the same. The traditional institutions did have this strange conception that people had the right to life, and that reflected itself in the emergence of various kinds of social welfare systems. People somehow couldn't get it into their heads that they had no right to life, and, instead of accepting the instruction provided to them by the science of the new economics (which had the certainty of the laws of gravitation, they were informed), they concluded that if we have no right to live, then you have no right to rule. The result was labor struggles and organization, the rise of the Chartist movement, and other threats to authority. Fortunately, the science is flexible and was soon adapted to permit measures to alleviate the grimmest hardships of the market system, merging it with residues of traditional institutions and later something like the welfare state, taking different forms in different societies.

Now of course, this new doctrine of modern capitalism ("no rights, just what you get in the market") – the rulers never accepted that for themselves. What they actually adopted is what we might call a "really existing free market doctrine" – which means market discipline for the poor and the weak, but plenty of state protection and subsidy for the rich and the privileged. In the United States, the weakness of traditional institutions created, or helped to create at least, the climate in which these harsh rules could be applied to an unusual degree. I don't want to suggest that the US is *sui generis*, but it's a little more in that direction than most other industrial societies for historical reasons. The political institutions of American society were quite consciously designed, and it makes sense to look back at the thinking, the very articulate thinking, of the people who designed them – the framers of the Constitution.

The most influential among those, as everyone knows, was James Madison, an important political thinker, who laid out the principles of governance very clearly, primarily in the debates at the Constitutional Convention in 1787. He emphasized there that the prime responsibility of the government is "to protect the minority of the opulent against the majority." Democracy he regarded as a threat that has to be diminished for that reason. Madison was no fool – he saw that there would be an increase in "the proportion of those who will labor under all the hardships of life, and secretly sigh for a more equal distribution of its blessings," and he already saw signs of the "symptoms of a leveling spirit," which give "warning of the future danger." The problem he faced in designing the constitutional system was to find a way "to secure the rights of property," meaning the privileged personal right to property, "against the danger from an equality of universality of suffrage, vesting complete power over property in hands without a share in it." Those "without property, or the hope of acquiring it," he reflected many years later, towards the end of his life, "cannot be expected to sympathize sufficiently with its rights, to be safe depositories of power over them."

Now, Madison's perspective was different from that of his friend, Jefferson, one of the few radical democrats in the crowd. Jefferson warned against the "aristocrats," those who "fear and distrust the people, and wish to draw all powers from them into the hands of the higher classes." He contrasted them with the "democrats," who "identify with the people, have confidence in them, cherish and consider them as the honest and safe... depository of the public interest," if not always "the most wise." Madison felt differently. The people, he felt, were not safe depositories of "the permanent interests of the country," because they would not sufficiently sympathize with the rights of property. So Madison insisted that political power must be in the hands of what he called "the more capable set of men" who come from and represent "the wealth of the nation." And his convictions prevailed – the Constitutional Convention was nearly unanimous in support of them, and that's become conventional. Of course, Madison was thinking of England (that was the model of the day), and he pointed out that if universal suffrage were granted, landed proprietors might be subjected to what we nowadays call agrarian reform. And in the new society that was being designed, he felt that it was necessary to ward off the danger of that injustice by restricting democracy in various ways.

It may be worth mentioning that in the first major study of political theory, his *Politics*, Aristotle discussed the same dilemma: in a society with concentrated wealth, democratic choice would infringe on the rights of property owners. Aristotle's solution was to reduce inequality by what we would call "welfare state measures." Facing the same dilemma, Madison chose to reduce democracy. And the constitutional system reflects that decision.

What Madison sought, some contemporary scholars argue, was a fragmented society with no hope of fraternity, equality or community, a political system designed to minimize citizen participation. The twentieth-century version is that the "meddlesome outsiders" can make their occasional choices among the "responsible men." At the Constitutional Convention, Madison's ideas prevailed. They were articulated with great clarity by his colleague John Jay, President of the Convention and first Chief Justice of the Supreme Court. His favorite maxim was that "those who own the country ought to govern it." That is, politics not only is, but ought to be, "the shadow cast on society by big business." Well, a lot has changed in 200 years, but these principles have remained in force, though they are continually adapted. Legal historian Jennifer Nedelsky argues that the Madisonian legacy helps to explain the weakness of the democratic tradition in the US and its failure to deal with the interpenetration of economic and political power. That's not quite right, I believe. It really has succeeded in dealing with that problem, but in a very specific way – by sanctifying and privileging the rights of those who own the country. That is what is meant by democracy in actual usage, and that's why you get these apparent paradoxes.

I should say that this picture of the Madisonian system is unfair to its founder. Like Smith and Jefferson, Madison was a pre-capitalist figure. His roots were in the Enlightenment and therefore, like the others, he was anti-capitalist in spirit – strongly so. The wealthy he had in mind were aristocrats who, he expected, would act as what he called "enlightened statesmen" and "benevolent philosophers" for the good of everyone. Well, he quickly discovered otherwise, and apparently with some shock. Within a few years, he found that the opulent minority were abusing the power he had handed over to them, and that they were acting in the way that Adam Smith had described – namely by following what Smith called "the vile maxim of the masters of mankind, all for ourselves and nothing for other people." Those are the guiding principles that we are taught to admire and revere, as traditional values are eroded under unremitting attack. Watching this, 200 years ago, Madison deplored what he called "the daring depravity of the times," as the "stockjobbers will become the praetorian band of the government – at once its tool and its tyrant; bribed by its largesse, and overawing it by clamors and combinations." It's pretty hard to improve on that description as we turn to the present.

There are people who expressed a much richer conception of democracy, and different values and attitudes. Some of them are very well known, say, John Dewey again, or Bertrand Russell. Russell disagreed with Dewey on a great many things, but agreed with him on what he called the "humanistic conception," or, to quote Dewey, the belief that "the ultimate aim of production" is not production of goods, but of "free human beings associated with one another on terms of equality." The goal of education, as Russell saw it, is "to give a sense of the value of things other than domination," to help create "wise citizens of a free community" in which both liberty and "individual creativeness" will flourish, and working people will be the masters of their fate, not tools of production. Illegitimate structures of coercion have to be unraveled – the central one, again in Dewey's words, being domination by "business for private profit through private control of banking, land, industry, reinforced by command of the press, press agents and other means of publicity and propaganda." Unless that's achieved, democratic forms lack substantive content. People will work "not freely and intelligently, but for the sake of the work earned," a condition that he said is "illiberal and immoral." Accordingly, industry has to be changed from "a feudalistic to a democratic social order" based on workers' control and free association. That's in the general range of a style of thought that also includes, along with many anarchists, guild socialists like G.D.H. Cole and left anti-Bolshevik Marxists like Anton Pannekoek, Rosa Luxemburg and others. Russell's views were quite similar in this regard.

These problems were the very focus of Dewey's thought and direct engagement. He is the leading American social philosopher of the twentieth century, and he was straight out of mainstream America, as American as apple pie. It is therefore of some interest that the ideas he expressed, not many years ago, would be regarded today, and in much of the intellectual culture, as outlandish or even anti-American, to use one of the terms that's been borrowed from totalitarian cultures.

It is useful to recognize how sharp and dramatic is the clash of values between this humanistic conception and the kind that we're taught to admire today. So you go from somebody like, say, Adam Smith (a pre-capitalist figure who stressed sympathy and solidarity, the goal of liberty with equality, and the basic human right to fulfilling work and a fair share of the product) to the values that are expressed by people who, often shamelessly, invoke Smith's name today. Let's put aside the more vulgar performances and turn to somebody you can take more seriously, like Nobel Prize-winning economist James Buchanan, who is a leading libertarian, in the American sense of the word. He states the following principle as an authoritative fact: "Any person's ideal situation is one that allows him full freedom of action and inhibits the behavior of others so as to force adherence to his own desires. That is to say, each person seeks mastery over a world of slaves." Smith would have regarded such a thought as pathological, as would Wilhelm von Humboldt, John Stuart Mill or anyone associated with the classical liberal tradition. But that is everyone's fondest dream – if you hadn't noticed it for yourself, and if you think it is not, you're wrong, because economic theory demonstrates it.

We hear a very different voice when we turn to the authentic Enlightenment and classical liberalism, or to serious modern commentators, or, still more interesting in my opinion, to the independent working-class press, which flourished from the mid-nineteenth century until it was finally destroyed by private power not so long ago. The nineteenth-century journals (which, again, are rarely studied) were run by what were called factory girls, young women from the farms, Irish immigrant artisans, and other working people. Their press condemned the "degradation and the loss of that self-respect, which had made the mechanics and laborers the pride of the world," as free people were forced to sell themselves, not what they produced, becoming "menials" and "humble subjects" of "despots" under wage slavery, not very different from the chattel slavery of Southern plantations, they felt. They described the destruction of "the spirit of free institutions," with working people reduced to a "state of servitude" in which they "see a moneyed aristocracy hanging over us like a mighty avalanche threatening annihilation to every man who dares to question their right to enslave and oppress the poor and unfortunate." They bitterly condemned what they called "the new spirit of the age: gain wealth forgetting all but self," a demeaning and shameful doctrine that no decent person could tolerate. Particularly dramatic, and again relevant to the current onslaught against democracy and human rights, was the attack on high culture that they deplored under the new spirit of the age. The factory girls, mechanics and others were used to spending their time reading classics; they were part of high culture. And that persisted. I can remember this from my own childhood among the working class communities in New York City, where immersion in literature, the arts, science, and so on was considered natural for unemployed working people. Driving out all that from people's minds was no small task. It's an achievement that you have to respect.

Going back to the working class press, "they who work in the mills ought to own them," they wrote, incidentally without the benefit of any radical intellectuals. In that way, they would overcome the "monarchical principles" that were taking root "on democratic soil." Years later, that became a rallying cry for the organized labor movement. At the 1893 convention of the American Federation of Labor, which belongs to the more conservative wing of the labor movement, Henry Demarest Lloyd gave what labor historian David Montgomery calls a "clarion call." He declared that the "mission of the labor movement is to free mankind from the superstitions and sins of the market, and to abolish the poverty which is the fruit of those sins. That goal can be attained by extending to the direction of the economy the principles of democratic politics." "It is by the people who do the work that the hours of labor, the conditions of employment, the division of the produce is to be determined." "It is by the workers themselves," Lloyd continued, that "the captains of industry are to be chosen, and chosen to be servants, not masters. It is for the welfare of all that the coordinated labor of all must be directed... This is democracy."

Well, those are values and insights that have only recently been suppressed, and they can be recovered.

These values would have seemed quite natural to the founders of classical liberalism. If you look at Adam Smith's sharp attack on the division of labor – not what one usually reads, but it is there – he attacked it because the division of labor would turn human beings into the most "stupid and ignorant" creatures that could be imagined. Therefore, "in any civilized society," the government would have to do something to stop this. It's intolerable to a pre-capitalist Enlightenment figure like Smith, as it was to de Tocqueville and others. De Tocqueville asks, "what can be expected of a man who has spent twenty years of his life making heads for pins?" "The art advances, the artisan recedes," he said, which is why he opposed inequality of condition and the threat of the manufacturing aristocracy. And it's taken a lot of work for the principles of Ricardo and Malthus and the rest to win this "everlasting battle for the minds of men" and drive these thoughts from the mind – though not very far, I believe.

Dewey and Russell are two of the major twentieth-century inheritors of this rich tradition, which also includes a lot of liberal, anarchist, and left Marxist thought. But I think, most vividly, it's captured both in the writings and in the inspiring struggles of men and women, as they sought to maintain and expand the sphere of freedom and justice in the face of this new despotism of state-supported private power, which they understood well enough. And it is worth remembering that this private power is tyrannical and totalitarian – it's long been understood. The intellectual origins of these institutions have been studied by Harvard University legal historian Morton Horwitz, in standard works. He points out that early in this century, when corporations were granted their extraordinary rights, there was a great deal of fascination with corporate entities – that is, social organisms that had rights over and above mere individuals, a sharp attack on fundamental principles of classical liberalism. These ideas grew from more or less the same neo-Hegelian soil, and they took three major forms, one being Bolshevism, the other fascism, and the third, modern corporations, which were granted extensive rights by courts and lawyers, often with the support of the progressives, reflecting those same attitudes. Two of those systems have succumbed; the third not only remains, but is expanding its sway and dominance. It's an extreme form of unaccountable tyranny and totalitarianism. It works in different ways, but is similar in its roots and functioning to the other outgrowths of these conceptions.

There are plenty of divisions and conflicts within the world of unaccountable concentrated power, but there is similarity in general conceptions. Quasi-governmental institutions are developing around them, designed in large measure to protect the wealthy and powerful from market discipline, and to socialize cost and risk. That is, or should be, familiar. But their role in establishing the Madisonian principles in a new guise has been much less noticed, and I think it is quite fundamental to understanding the world that's taking shape around us.

Question and Answer Session

Question: *You have talked about the problems of democracy in the so-called capitalist countries, but you did not say anything about the socialist countries. Do you give any credit to their achievements in the field of social justice? Now that they have collapsed and that only capitalism remains, is capitalism really the way of the future, the end of history?*

Chomsky: Well, to respond to this, one has to recognize that the terms of political discourse don't have much meaning anymore. So we can't talk of socialist and capitalist countries, because there aren't any, at least in any very clear or recognizably traditional sense of these terms. Neither socialist, nor capitalist. There certainly aren't any capitalist industrial societies. I mean, a good part of the Third World is capitalist, that's why it's the Third World, but the rich and powerful countries have never accepted it, that goes from England up to the newly industrializing countries in East Asia, and, dramatically so, the US. They have never accepted capitalism; they are all state-capitalist countries with a very powerful and significant state component.

With regard to socialist countries, there certainly aren't any. And, in fact, nobody understood that better than Lenin and Trotsky. Whatever you think of them (and I don't think much myself), they were orthodox Marxists, and did not regard socialism as possible in this backward, peasant, impoverished country. They were carrying out a kind of holding action in the hope (well, you know the routine) that the iron laws of history would lead to a revolution in the advanced capitalist world, which meant Germany. But revolution didn't come in Germany, and they were left in charge of this pre-capitalist, pre-industrial society (from their point of view). Lenin moved on to a form of state capitalism. The first step that Lenin and Trotsky took was to demolish every working class organization in Russia, consciously, because that was the right thing to do, again, from their point of view. There was no place for factory councils and Soviets in this pre-industrial society – it was capitalism, according to the routine, that was supposed to industrialize and democratize, and that sort of thing. In the other so-called socialist countries, it was the same. It's striking that all these countries later called themselves socialist and democratic. So they were the best democracies and the most socialist countries. In the West, everybody ridiculed the claim to democracy, but western propaganda loved the equally ridiculous claim to socialism as a technique for undermining socialism. Therefore, the idea that these were socialist countries was not only accepted, but – for obvious reasons – became the dominant principle in the West. On the other hand, the equally ridiculous claim that they were democratic was laughed at. Both claims are equally absurd, but the claim that they were socialist has caught on. When both of the world's two major propaganda systems agree on something, it's kind of difficult for ordinary individuals to extricate themselves from it. So there were no big moves towards socialism. There are moves towards social democracy, and sometimes considerably more all over the world, welfare systems, collectives, all sorts of things, but they are scattered here and there, and when they really try to reach a large scale, they get smashed. Probably the most advanced case was the Spanish Revolution of 1936, which was jointly attacked by the communists, fascists and liberal democracies. It wasn't until they wiped out that plague of freedom and socialism that they got back to the less significant question of who picks up the spoils. So the question really can't be answered as it is posed.

On the other hand, if you look at the anti-socialist, anti-democratic societies of eastern Europe, they had some achievements of social justice. In the western industrial world, the standard story about the collapse of the Soviet Union is not just that it committed crimes, but that it was very inefficient and didn't work. Well, by what standards didn't it work? The usual argument is, look at eastern Europe and western Europe – at how advanced western Europe is and how poor eastern Europe is. You'll see what a failure eastern Europe was. That makes about as much sense as if somebody were to look at the schools in Cambridge, Massachusetts and say what a failure the kindergartens are – just see how much quantum physics these kids know as compared to how much they know when they come out of MIT. This is the same argument. If you have to compare two systems of development, you have to start at a point at which they are more or less alike. And the last time that eastern and western Europe were alike is the fifteenth century. After that, they diverge, with eastern Europe becoming the regional "Third World." And that decline, relative to the West, continued up to the First World War. For a meaningful comparison, you want to compare countries that are more or less at par when the two experiments began in the twentieth century: say Russia and Brazil, Bulgaria and Guatemala, or something like that. Those would be more or less fair comparisons; actually, unfair to Russia because Brazil and Guatemala had many advantages. There is a good reason why nobody carries out that comparison. It teaches absolutely the wrong lesson. It tells you that however monstrous the eastern European command economies might have been, what the West has imposed on the rest of the world is much worse. For more than eighty percent of the population of Brazil, eastern Europe would look like a paradise. And that's something that people are not allowed to think about. It takes a remarkable amount of brainwashing to get the whole West, almost without exception, not to see this. Even the left can't hear it when you point it out. But it's pretty elementary – as elementary as the comparison of the Cambridge kindergartens to MIT.

In answer to your question, did they achieve something – yes. That's why eastern Europe is not called the Third World anymore. It's called the Second World. It used to be the Third World, it's not anymore. Well, something happened there. It's now being driven back to the Third World, consciously. That's what the Cold War was about. It was to get them back to the Third World. They achieved certain goals, in a brutal and cruel fashion: they did industrialize the society, create a high degree of education and health by Third World standards, and were relatively egalitarian as contemporary societies go. In fact, up until the 1960s, the primary fear of the West was that eastern Europe was too successful. If you look at the internal records, it's quite different from what the intellectuals talk about. US and British leaders were worried that it looked too successful. That was the real problem.

Coming to the second part of the question, there isn't any capitalism, so it can't be the wave of the future. Is state-supported transnational corporate capitalism the wave of the future? Well, if you let it be, yes. Nazism would have been the wave of the future if you let it be. But there's no particular reason why anybody should agree to that. It's a monstrous system from every point of view, a failure from a social and economic point of view, and unviable and unsustainable, at least in anything like its current form, not to speak of the fundamental defects of the system – to put it mildly – that were clear enough to poor working people in the early days of the industrial revolution.

3. The Vicissitudes of Democracy: Part 2*

Yesterday, I was talking about James Madison's vision for the country, and his distress shortly afterwards, when he saw the fate of the constitutional system he had devised. I recalled that in Madison's pre-capitalist vision, power was to be put in the hands of more capable people, the wealthy, but they were not supposed to act as gangsters and robbers. They were supposed to be benevolent gentlemen and wise philosophers and act for the benefit of all, while of course understanding that the prime responsibility of the government is "to protect the minority of the opulent against the majority," and to ensure that property rights are privileged. In principle, all people (at least, free white males) were to have the same rights, but property owners were granted special rights, misleadingly called "rights of property." They were expected to understand that, but in an enlightened fashion. And he was concerned, as I mentioned, with the threat of democracy. That's the basis on which the modern democratic states are established. They are founded on the basis of the threat of democracy, and the need to contain it, and to ensure that the prime responsibility of the government is fulfilled.

Madison, as I said, was concerned about the levelling spirits among the growing number of people who "labor under all the hardships of life, and secretly sigh for more equal distribution of its blessings." And then he lamented when he saw that the powerful behaved in the way one would expect, deploring "the daring depravity of the times" as the rising business classes became at once the "tools and tyrants" of the government, overwhelming it with their power and benefiting from its bribes and largesse. I mentioned this because these are the standard

* Lecture delivered at the Delhi School of Economics on 13 January 1996.

http://dx.doi.org/10.11647/OBP.0050.03

views of classical liberalism – anti-capitalist in spirit and in character, very much in favor of insisting upon equality of condition, and also opposed to the division of labor which will destroy people, critical of capital export, and nuanced with regard to trade. There is a big difference between the actual ideals of classical liberalism with their Enlightenment roots and the modern version, called neo-liberalism, which is virtually the opposite in most important respects. This is why the early Marx drew quite heavily on the French and German Enlightenment and also on Romantic philosophy, which was imbued with much the same spirit.

Apart from the stateliness of Madison's rhetoric, what he said about the rising business classes as the tools and tyrants of government, and the daring depravity of the times is a good description of Washington or London or other capitals today. To see the way it's described in modern terms, I'll just quote from *BusinessWeek*, reviewing the year since the electoral triumph of the Gingrich army in November 1994. *BusinessWeek* reports that most CEOs feel that "the 104th Congress represents a milestone for business: Never before have so many goodies been showered so enthusiastically on America's entrepreneurs," who are by now quite openly designing the legislation, without even the usual pretenses. The number of corporate lobbyists has exploded. There is no secret about it anymore.

The headline of the *BusinessWeek* article is "Return to the trenches." In other words, yes, we've got more goodies than ever before in history, but it's not enough, you can get more. The article goes on to describe "the more" that we've got to get, now that we've got so much. The first thing is a reduction of taxes on financial gains – that's extremely important in countries where taxes are collected. For the wealthiest one percent of the population, financial gains are about half their income. So half their income has to be completely exempt from taxes. Now, this is supposed to be necessary to stimulate investment. But that doesn't make any sense from an economic point of view. If you want to stimulate investment, the obvious way to do it is to put money in the pockets of working people, so they can consume and increase demand, and that would stimulate investment. That's particularly true when the country is absolutely awash in capital. It's not that there is any shortage of investment capital, it's just that there is weak demand and there are better ways to make money (by financial speculation and so on), and promoting those can't help to increase investment.

The real purpose is quite different – it is to increase the Third World, to stimulate the development of a society of the Third World structural type. That is, to increase the enormous inequality that has been growing steadily since the mid-1970s, but spectacularly so since the Reagan takeover in the 1980s. The level of inequality in the US is now back to what it was around the 1920s – right before the big crash in 1929. By 1980, which was the turning point, the level of inequality in the US was comparable to the worst in the industrial world – it was among the worst, but not off the spectrum. Now, it's completely beyond any other industrial society, as is the proportion of people living under conditions of poverty, the incidence of starvation among children and the elderly, and other standard indices which are familiar to the Third World. Those conditions are being established, of course, at higher levels, since it's a rich society. But the conditions are structurally quite the same, and the point of the reduction of taxes on financial gains is simply to accelerate these developments. It's striking when you look at it case by case. Take New York City – the richest city in the world. Over forty percent of children live below the official poverty level, which means they are deprived of any possibility of a productive future life. The level of inequality in New York City is the same as in Guatemala, which is the worst in the world for any country where there are statistics.

Guatemala is an interesting case, because you may recall that they had a brief experiment with democracy until 1954, when it was overthrown by a US government-backed military coup. At that time the US was going to turn Guatemala into a showplace for capitalism and democracy. A couple of hundred thousand corpses later, Guatemala has perhaps the worst inequality in the world and child starvation. And yes, tremendous wealth. It is a showcase of a kind, and New York City now has approximately the same level of inequality.

The second major task for which business has to go back to the trenches is deregulation. It is important – it imposes very severe costs on the population and, of course, on future generations. Because deregulation has obvious costs, but it's good for short-term profits. And if there is trouble, you can go to the taxpayer to bail you out. That's taken for granted. In fact, if you look at the cases and see what happens, deregulation is being done in a very intelligent fashion. They are not dismantling the system piece by piece – they want to destroy it all at once. So the technique that is being used is to introduce what economists call cost-benefit analysis, risk analysis. As any honest economist will tell you, that it is something you can't do. The situation is much too complex. And you can't carry out any sensible measure of things like cost-benefit analysis in a complex system. That's very significant. Because the current legislation is that before any regulatory legislation is introduced, it must be demonstrated that the gains are not exceeded by the cost, in terms of growth or profits or whatever. Any corporate lawyer with half his brain functioning can keep the courts tied up for years trying to work out what that means. This essentially means no regulation, by the highest scientific principles. Of course, to carry any of this out requires a huge government bureaucracy. But that's no problem, that's not funded. So yes, we have enormous bureaucratic costs, but we don't fund them, so they can't be carried out. We impose tests on regulatory processes which can't possibly be met. This means the system collapses. Now, when it collapses, it leads to disasters, but there is an answer to that too, you turn to the public to bail you out, that's what happens in case after case.

The Savings and Loan crisis in the US was a perfect example of that. In the early 1980s, the government deregulated these Savings and Loan banks, but it also gave them incentives to carry out very high-risk loans, by increasing the insurance for the banks. It doesn't take a genius to figure out what will happen – huge scandals, great profits, collapse, hundreds of billions of dollars of losses, but that's simply passed over to the taxpayer. Another example is right in the works now; the securities markets are being deregulated. The head of the Securities and Exchange Commission under Reagan, a great liberal who was in charge during the 1987 crash, points out this is going to be a disaster. What they are doing is reducing liabilities, freeing brokers from liabilities for fraudulent practices when they sell stocks, which is just an invitation to disaster. The Congressional Budget Office, which is a very conservative outfit, estimates that in order to deal with the fraud that is going to follow from this they will have to double or triple the case load against the Securities and Exchange Commission. Again, a huge bureaucracy. But that's no problem because they are cutting the budget for it, so they won't be able to do these things. And then when the collapse comes, very simple – you just go back to the taxpayer to bail you out.

That just happened again in Mexico. Mexico was what is called an economic miracle: disaster for the majority of the population, but a dream for the rising number of billionaires who were being given state assets for a fraction of their value under privatization, and for foreign investors (mostly speculators). And when the bubble bursts, as obviously it is going to – very simply, go to the American taxpayer who will end up paying 30-40 billion dollars' worth of pay-offs. Not to the Mexicans – it doesn't go to them. It goes to the investment bankers and speculators to protect them from losses. They incidentally happen to be the same kind of people who, by and large, staff Clinton's cabinet. And so on, in case after case.

There is a dramatic case right now. In the middle of this frenzy about deregulation, last December the Commerce Department in the US had to close down Georges Bank. Georges Bank is the richest fishing area in the world. It had to be virtually closed to commercial fishing. The reason was that, in the early 1980s, under the excitement about deregulation, they deregulated the fishing industry. But they did it in the way it is done in "really existing free markets": they also gave the fishing industry subsidies to increase the fishing. So you subsidize the fishing industry and you deregulate it, and again it doesn't take a genius to figure out what will happen – over-fishing. They destroyed the ground fish, and now there is a danger of wiping out the edible fish. Today, New England is importing cod from Norway. It is just like Australia importing kangaroos from Central Asia. But nobody can understand why. Something went wrong. Actually, one person did understand why – the Governor of Massachusetts, William Weld, a rising star of conservatism. He went to Washington, hat in hand, asking for a federal handout to pay the costs at the expense of the taxpayer. His argument was that the government should declare this a national disaster, which means that federal funds then pour in. And as to why it is a national disaster, he found some scientists who were willing to tell him that some predatory fish had probably come to Georges Bank and was eating all the ground fish. He said that they hadn't been able to find it yet, but they were pretty sure it was there, so therefore the taxpayer ought to pay off the cost – because it is a national disaster.

This goes on, in case after case. The Reagan administration bailed out the Continental Illinois Bank, the biggest nationalized bank in American history. They got into trouble, and the taxpayer bailed them out. This is a standard feature of neo-liberal economics. Take Chile, which is hailed as one of the greatest economic miracles in history since the Pinochet takeover in the 1970s. It was an economic miracle run by the smartest economists around, the "Chicago boys" as they were called, who followed all the rules. They were able to do this very easily, because the fascist dictatorship was able to murder, torture, and imprison those who objected to the human consequences. That made it easy to carry out the neo-liberal agenda, and it was considered a huge economic success until 1982, when everything collapsed, and Chile had the worst economic disaster in fifty years. At that point, libertarian think-tanks simply advised the government to take over the assets of all the failed banks, and industries, and so on, which they did, and it turned out that the Chilean government acquired more control over the economy than at the peak of the Allende government. Until, of course, the taxpayer had resolved the crisis, at which point the giveaway began again, and you return to the principles of neo-liberalism. It's an awful scam, but that's exactly what you'd expect when power is transferred, more and more, into the hands of those who have every reason to make law and government the combination of the rich against the poor – exactly what's happening. So, that's deregulation.

The third major policy to be pursued is devolution – reducing power down from the federal government to the state level. There have been philosophical debates about federalism versus central government, and so on and so forth, and the idea of devolution is supposed to be that the conservatives believe in moving power to the people, and that means getting it down to the state level. Well, that's just shameless cynicism as everyone knows, but nobody will say. The point of giving power to the state (say, by giving block grants to the state governments instead of specified funding for health, and education, and so on, at the federal level) is very straightforward. State governments are much weaker than the federal government, which means that even medium-sized business can play one state against the other: say, threaten to transfer across state borders if you don't give them some extra benefits. Only the really big guys can play that game with national states (say, by moving from Mexico to Poland unless some benefits are given), but moving from Massachusetts to Tennessee is quite easy.

Take the Raytheon Corporation, which is the biggest employer in Massachusetts and is part of what's called the defense industry – meaning, the public pays for it but the profits are privatized. The only defense that anybody can detect is defense of the minority of the opulent against the majority at home – that is apparently the function. It's part of a system where the public pays the cost of high-tech industry. Anyway, Raytheon recently informed the state of Massachusetts that it would move to Tennessee unless it got more tax benefits and subsidies. The legislature passed laws that exempt the defense industry from taxes, even more so than before, and gave other amenities amounting to 80 billion dollars a year. That's the kind of thing that a middle-sized business can do. As I say, only the big corporations can do that with national states. That's exactly the point of devolution: if you can devolve power down to the state level, you can be more confident that the limited funding going to education, health, shelter, transport and other economically irrational things will not trickle down (as it sometimes does) to people who need it, but will be transferred by some combination of regressive fiscal measures and outright subsidies into the very deep pockets of the opulent minorities. That's devolution in the real world.

The next thing that has to be pursued is total reform – change the legal system. That means elimination of liability for criminal action by corporations, and that's important because they carry out plenty of criminal action. In fact, the biggest corporate funder for the Gingrich army happens to be Philip Morris Corporation, the biggest tobacco firm, which needs protection from its many millions of victims. It is killing people on a scale that the whole narco-trafficking industry in the world can't come close to. There are all sorts of legal cases demanding compensation for this, and the idea is to cut them off, similarly to other forms of corporate crime. Not only must private tyranny be publicly subsidized, its activities also have to be decriminalized – this is total reform.

The next priority is a very interesting one – it is health care. Business is running back to the trenches to change the health care system. As I mentioned yesterday, the US is unusual in a lot of ways for historical reasons. One of the effects of this somewhat different history is that the US is the only major industrial country without any comprehensive national health care system. In the 1960s, two programs were introduced – Medicare and Medicaid – to provide health support to the elderly and the poor. The idea now is to get rid of those programs. The nature of the reforms being introduced has been described pretty accurately in a headline of the *Wall Street Journal*. The headline says, "Unequal treatment – Medicare Bill would end egalitarian approach," and the story reports that the wealthy stand to gain, the poor may be hurt and there will be trade-offs for the middle class. This is more or less true, but you have to understand what these words mean. First of all, it's not that the poor *may* be hurt, they are almost certain to be hurt. That's the point of it – to eliminate support for medical aid to the poor. Approximately 40 million lack any insurance at all. They are dumped. There are dumping grounds for them called public hospitals. The poor and the uninsured are taken care of in public hospitals, but public hospitals have to be eliminated. That's part of the system, and in fact, the same day, in the *New York Times* the lead headline was "Public Hospitals Facing Deep Cuts in Medicare Bill." The subhead reports that there will be "less for teaching programs and for services to the poor." Some may have to close down, and others will lose resources, because we don't want these dumping grounds around. These are disposable people, in the Third World sense. It doesn't make sense to keep them alive. Therefore, cutting back the limited medical aid that they have makes a good deal of sense. Any economist can explain that to you, and in the Third World domains of the West, say Latin America, that is done all the time. So it is the poor who will be hurt – not *may* be hurt.

As for the middle class, it is getting a trade-off. The term "middle class" does not mean the people around the median. It means the almost very rich, but not quite very rich. So the middle class is all those right below the top, but well above the median. And for them, there will be a trade-off. So the wealthy will gain, and for the ones below them, there will be trade-offs. The poor, which are a large majority of the people – they'll be hurt. Furthermore, the health care system which remains mostly for the rich is being handed over much more than before to private businesses. And as Milton Friedman – or anyone else sensible – says, they are not benevolent organizations. They are in the business of making profits. Now, if you are a health-maintenance management organization, and you want to make profits, what you do is micro-manage the doctors. Introduce extensive levels of managerial bureaucracy to make sure that the patients get the least possible care and attention, and at minimal costs. You don't need to go to a school of management to understand that. That's the point of micro-management, and the costs are enormous. There are all sorts of costs which wouldn't be there in a rational system – and aren't there in the national health care system, say, of Canada next door. For one thing, a large part of the health cost which will increase is just high profits. Another is the high level of bureaucratization, micro-management, complex accounting procedures, and so on. Right now, the administrative costs and profits of the HMOs (Health Management Organizations) are about seven times as high as the comparable costs of Medicare or any public system anywhere. There is a huge amount of advertising – open the newspaper in the US and you will see big advertisements for joining some HMO. Well those are costs – of course, they are not real costs to the corporation because advertisements are tax free, so the public pays part of the cost of the propaganda. Another cost is lobbying, which is also tax deductible. So the lobbying which gets these things through is partially paid by the public, who suffer from it. Then there are huge salaries, stock options, and so on. Well, all these are ways of transferring costs. They don't cut costs, they transfer costs from the hands of some private power to the public, and that's understood.

There is a conservative commission called the Bipartisan National Leadership Coalition, chaired by a couple of ex-presidents, which estimates that the current costs in the government health programs are going to take 67 billion dollars out of wages or income, hitting mostly the poorer people because it takes a much bigger percentage from them. They also estimate that these programs may raise the number of uninsured to about 54 million or so individuals in the next seven years. It will be 46 million with no cuts, which is bad enough. Well, those are among the costs and they are extreme. Medicare has been the major support so far for nursing homes for the elderly, etc. If Medicare disappears, the elderly will have nowhere to go unless private families take care of them. Right now, there are laws which say that if you put your parents under nursing care, you can apply for federal support without losing your personal assets – that means your house, car, etc., won't be taken. If that legislation is eliminated, people will be faced with agonizing choices like, do I lose my home and send my children out in the streets in order to keep my parents from dying? But that is not the kind of thing that counts when you use the yardstick of economic rationality and other forms of lunacy that we are told to admire. Well, that's a part of the cost-shifting that goes on, which will give figures showing that medical costs are being controlled, but only by transferring them over to the public.

Take deregulation, again. Deregulation has already allowed increased pollution – so you can dump toxic wastes, and somebody else pays the costs. By dumping wastes you damage sewage and water systems. How do you deal with it? You raise the cost of using water. But that simply transfers the cost to private families and individuals and takes it away from the industrial polluters. Deregulation is then described as being economically very efficient – look how it's cutting costs, and so on. In fact, it's just shifting the cost, in a highly regressive fashion, to people who pay it themselves. This has become so brazen that the new legislation requires the taxpayers to reimburse industrial polluters who have created toxic wastes and have been compelled to clean them up to meet federal standards. They now have to be reimbursed by the taxpayer for the cost of cleaning up the toxic wastes they have created. And so it goes on.

The City and State of New York have announced big tax cuts. If you take a look at them, almost all go to business and the wealthy. But tax cuts are good for the economy. The only trouble is while they have introduced tax cuts, they have also introduced tax hikes to compensate for the tax cuts, except that they don't called them tax hikes – they call them reduction in subsidies for mass transportation and education. This is a funny notion, that when people's money goes to enable them to have a transportation system and a school, it is a subsidy. What happens when we reduce subsidies to mass transportation and public education? What happens is that the costs of mass transportation, which were already very high, get higher – they just shot up by twenty percent. But those costs are paid by poor people. People who drive limousines don't care if subway rates go up. But the children who have to get to school and poor people trying to get to work – they care a lot. If costs go up at city colleges, poor people are hit. The rich are sending their kids to private institutions. So all this is another radically regressive shift in taxes. It's called a tax cut, but it is really tax shifting, taxes becoming more regressive than they already are. There is a lot of talk about flat taxes, overlooking the fact that they are already flat, and they've been flat since the Reagan years, if you take a look at the whole tax system. So making them flat simply means making them radically regressive, instead of just very regressive. All this is very familiar in India's own history: sixty-five years ago the British had to raise funds for the Indian government and had a choice of raising income tax or salt tax; you know the choice they made, and that is exactly the same thing. Income tax hurts the rich, salt tax just hurts the poor – that's the kind of tax you want, with consequences I'm sure you remember.

It is instructive to see how all this stuff is portrayed. Here is one example. The mayor of New York City (a well-known conservative) had a press conference in which he explained that the city is just not wealthy enough to support poor people anymore. The basis for that judgment, repeated as front-page story in the *New York Times*, was an investment report by JP Morgan Bank, the fifth largest financial institution in New York. JP Morgan was suffering from, I think, a mere 1.4 billion dollars in profit last year, and they came out with this report saying New York is not rich. So it's necessary to cut things like transport and education subsidies, care for the disabled and elderly, all this stuff. The headline under which this appeared was "Giuliani Sees Welfare Cuts Providing a Chance to Move." The article explains that

Giuliani's welfare cuts really are for the benefit of the poor: the cuts "enable them to move freely around the country." At last, they are liberated from their chains – homes to live in, food to eat, and medical care if they get sick – so they are free to go somewhere else. It's straight benevolence: free to move, the chains are gone! Well, that is one way to do it.

Turning to another example, there was a recent op-ed by a specialist at the Hoover Institute at Stanford (a very respectable and conservative academic institute) talking about the health care problem and describing a philosophical flaw in the President's position on health care. Why? Liberals favor a nationally-guaranteed level of benefits and redistribution of income through entitlements. Conservatives prefer to transfer power to the states in the belief that policies should be closer to the people. These are profound philosophical differences, he says. But for reasons I've already mentioned, no sane observer can fail to understand that when you move closer to the people, i.e., states, you are actually transferring power away from the people into the hands of private institutions that can manipulate and control the state. And if anyone is unable to understand this, he or she can turn to the report released the same day explaining that Fidelity, the biggest investment firm in Massachusetts, is demanding a cut in state taxes and warning that unless it gets even more subsidies it will move next door to Rhode Island, where it would have a much lower tax burden, though it wouldn't be so easy to move, say, to Zurich. Massachusetts capitulated, and that means tax rates increase for the poor, so that Fidelity can make use of the services of the city, but the poor people pay for it. That's called creating a better environment for business, being more economically rational and so on. And that's the philosophical difference.

There is one real success story – an economic miracle – in the US (not just Mexico or Brazil). It's the state of Wisconsin. That's the state that pioneered creative approaches to getting rid of welfare, eliminating all these horrors of a welfare state. And it is praised by liberals for its achievements. In fiscal 1994, the state of Wisconsin spent 1.16 billion dollars on what *BusinessWeek* calls "the goodies" showered on entrepreneurs – that whole array of subsidies and benefits. That kind of corporate welfare has grown astronomically since the 1970s, when the conservative experiment began. Meanwhile, the state economy has scarcely grown at all. Real wages have dropped for non-supervisory workers. They are now the lowest in the entire Midwest manufacturing region. The tax burden has shifted dramatically to individual households. But all these huge gifts to corporations have not led to any expansion of employment, and the reason is very simple: there are better ways to make money – speculation, mergers, and all kinds of things.

The day I left the US, there was a little news item in the back pages, which reported a study of educational expenditure in Wisconsin. It said that there has been a big increase in public funding for wealthy communities and sharp cutbacks for the working class and the poor. Well, that's an economic miracle – that's what the term means in its technical sense. Just about every place that's called an economic miracle has those properties – they are quite familiar throughout the Third World. Now we've got a couple of such miracles at home – New York, Wisconsin, and so on. There are, of course, similar tendencies at the national level, but it all gets sharply accentuated when you move down to the state level, where there are weaker public defenses against private power.

Let's go back to that *BusinessWeek* message, "back to the trenches, we haven't got enough." Who does that go to? Well, it goes to the 23,000 corporate lobbyists in Washington, as compared with less than 700 of them in 1970. That's one reflection of the massive attack on democracy and rights that has taken place during this period. The number of corporate lawyers has expanded at a similar rate. The business press is absolutely euphoric about what the *BusinessWeek* commentary calls "spectacular profits." Last year was the fourth straight year of double-digit profit growth. There was very little sales growth, and very little change in employment, but return on capital has skyrocketed, executive pay has gone up about sixty-six percent since 1980, and capital gains about the same. Just as I was about to leave the US, the record came up for 1995. The *New York Times* reported record profits, while real wages and benefits decline – so the frenzy continues.

As I left the city, I had to pick up some cash from the bank. So I went to the Bank of Boston, the biggest bank in Massachusetts, and picked up a little leaflet they had for people. Record net-income earnings, up by about twenty to twenty-five percent over 1994, which was a bumper year. They've just become the biggest foreign bank in Argentina. They quote the chief economist of the Bank of Boston saying the economy is doing just great – there is low growth, huge profits. Inflation is under control and "fortunately" wage increases have been remarkably restrained. That means they've declined, indeed median wages have been declining steadily since around 1980. The decline continued through the Clinton recovery – that's unprecedented. There's been an economic recovery in the last couple of years, growth has been faster than in the Reagan years, but the median real wages have kept going down. That's the "fortunate" fact, that they've been remarkably restrained. The *Wall Street Journal* called it "a welcome development of transcendent importance," no less. Labor costs in the US have reached the lowest level in the industrial world, next to England, where Thatcher did an even better job in crushing poor people. In 1985, they were the highest, but now they are the lowest next to England, so that's of transcendent importance.

All this has been happening at a time of spectacular profits, double-digit growth of profits, and so on. I should add that aside from the loss of income and wages, there is also much less security. Since 1980 or so, the number of workers under contracts has declined, unions have declined, and the number of temporary workers has shot up. One of the biggest employers in the US now is called Manpower Incorporated – its sales are temporary workers. People who don't get benefits, and don't need to be given a job tomorrow, and so on. In the technical literature, this lowering of wages and elimination of contracts is called "flexibility of labor markets," which is good for the health of the economy.

On the other hand, it's not that the government is being cut back. The taxes are just being shifted. So there are parts of the government that are going up. The biggest and most important one is the Pentagon. The Gingrich army and the Heritage Foundation (the right-wing libertarian foundation that more or less sets the agenda) have called for and have got an increase in the Pentagon budget. The Pentagon budget is roughly at Cold War levels in absolute terms, but it's going up. Not because the country is under any risk or threat – nobody can believe that. But because of the function of the Pentagon system, which is well understood. It is not studied in the academic literature, but it is well understood in the business community. In the late 1940s, business understood very well that, as *Fortune* magazine put it, high-tech industry cannot survive in an unsubsidized, competitive, free-enterprise economy. The government must do something about it. *BusinessWeek* added that the government must be the savior. The natural mechanism to save big business was the military system. There are many reasons for this, but one reason is that defense is easy to sell to the public – frighten the public and then they'll pay for it.

The first Secretary of the Air Force under Truman, a liberal Democrat, pointed out that the word to use is "security," not "subsidy." So when you give a subsidy to a high-tech industry you call it security, and that goes through the Pentagon system. It is kept away from any public control or public scrutiny, because it is secret, and has every possible advantage. It goes up under more statist elements like the Reaganites, just as protection did. Maybe the most dramatic example of this influence is Gingrich himself, who heads a conservative revolution. You can find many press reports on the new rise of conservatism in the US that focus on the fiery leader of the revolution, Newt Gingrich, who is full of enthusiasm about entrepreneurial values and how people want to get the nanny state off their back. Gingrich describes the Georgia county he represents as a Norman Rockwell world – Rockwell is a painter who paints happy middle-class people – "a Norman Rockwell world with fiber optic computers and jet planes," just a wonderful place – "A Suburban Eden Where the Right Rules," a *New York Times* headline tells us, and where "conservatism flowers among the malls," where happy people shop. That's what happens when you're a free entrepreneur, liberated from the nanny state. There is a little footnote to that, sort of in the background somewhere, which is that this very affluent district right outside of Atlanta gets more federal subsidies than any suburban county in the country, with the exception of the federal system itself (Arlington, Virginia, across the river from Washington, where the Pentagon and other federal agencies are located, and Brevard County, Florida, the home of the Kennedy Space Center). And the computers, fiber optics, and jet planes are also primarily a gift of the nanny state. The county's largest employer is Lockheed Corporation, which it would be inaccurate to describe as state-subsidized, since it is closer to a part of the federal government which happens to record private profits. It's really easy to talk about getting the nanny state out of your hair, to triumphantly proclaim libertarian values, and so forth, as long as you are feeding at the public trough. But it's not enough – back to the trenches.

In fact, things have reached a point where the concept of capitalism has disappeared from the business world. They don't understand it any more. You can see this if you read the business press, like the *Wall Street Journal*. A couple of weeks ago, it had a lead story about business strategies. It compared the business strategies of two different states, Virginia and Maryland. They had different approaches (just like India and Brazil), different methods of bringing in investment and having development. And the article talked about which approach is better, which one worked and which one did not. It turned out that for a while Maryland was better and now Virginia is better. Maryland had been banking on biotechnology, and genetic engineering, and the biology-based industries. And Virginia, which they said had a better business climate and more supportive individual entrepreneurs, was developing computers and telecommunications: Virginia is doing better, and that shows the values of capitalism, better business climates, and so on. Now, as it happens, Maryland and Virginia are the two states next to Washington, and if you read the story, it turns out that these investment efforts are not being made by Maryland and Virginia but by areas around Washington (suburbs of Washington). And the difference in business strategy is that Maryland was banking on putting its hand in the public pocket through the parts of the federal government that subsidize biology-based industries, while Virginia had the smarter idea of putting its hands into the deeper pockets of the part of the federal government which pays the costs of the high-tech industry – namely the defense system. Well, that turned out to be a better strategy, so the better technique for private enterprise is to make sure you smartly pick the public funds you're going to rob. That's regarded, without comment, as the way capitalism should work. And that is the way it does work. If you look back in history, that is the way it generally worked. All this continues and expands on and on.

There is a lot more to say about this, but I'm going to save time for discussion. Let me just say that this is not the first time we find ourselves in this situation. About a hundred years ago, William Morris, the famous British revolutionary socialist writer, told an Oxford audience that, "I know it is at present the received opinion that the competitive, or 'Devil take the hindmost', system is the last system of economy which the world will see; that it is perfection, and therefore finality has been reached in it; and it is doubtless a bold thing to fly in the face of this opinion, which I am told is held even by the most learned men." And he goes on to say that if history is really at an end as most learned men proclaim, then "civilization will die." But all of history tells us, he says, that it is not so. And despite what the learned men tell him he will continue to fly in the face of this opinion. And he was right. History was not over. There were continuing popular struggles, many achievements; the world is, in many ways, a much better place today than it was then.

That pattern has been repeated. In the 1920s again, in the US there was a belief that perfection had been reached, finality had come, with a utopia for the masters. But the masters and learned men turned out to be wrong – a couple of years later there was mass mobilization, coming close to worker takeover of factories, later moves into the welfare state system, and so on. And so it continues. There is still plenty of leeway for action; these human institutions are under control. If "the daring depravity of the times" does last, and history comes to an end, and civilization dies, we'll know exactly who is to blame – namely ourselves, because there is plenty that can be done about it.

Question and Answer Session

Question: *As you know, countries like India, China and Indonesia are competing for capital and hoping to become part of this wonderful system that you just described. California and other states are competing with them, too. But do you see any signs of popular struggle – a hope of democracy? Do you see any struggle emerging that we can gain some hope from?*

Chomsky: There are plenty of people like William Morris who don't accept the opinion of the most learned men. Sure, there are struggles all over the place. France just had big general strikes. The poorest country in the western hemisphere is Haiti, which had a remarkable example of democratization a couple of years ago. It is really an instructive lesson. This is a highly impoverished country – I was there at the height of the terror, and the poverty is incredible. You see it in India, but there it is everywhere. Incidentally, Haiti used to be a rich country – a source of a good deal of Europe's wealth. But now it's miserable and impoverished. A couple of years ago, to everyone's surprise, the general population (people in slums, peasants in the hills) had succeeded on their own in developing a vibrant and lively civil society with grassroots organizations, popular initiatives, and so on. A lot of it was impelled by liberation theology, which has had a big effect in the region. And to everyone's amazement, they managed to sweep their own president into office with quite a popular program. Of course, a coup came along and it got crushed. The US pretended to oppose it, but in fact backed it. Finally the US came back in and re-instituted the program that the population had thrown out. That was the condition under which the president was allowed to return: that he adopt the harsh neoliberal program of the defeated US candidate in the election, who received fourteen percent of the votes. That is what is now hailed as proof of Washington's awe-inspiring dedication to democracy. However, the Haitian population, despite three years of terror and lots of killings, are still resisting it. This is another country that has resisted structural adjustment, resisted it to the extent that the World Bank and the US government have started cutting off the aid they were giving. But Haiti is much too small to be able to resist. In France too, the working class and general public are not strong enough to resist on their own. Everywhere you look, there are these signs of resistance and they do involve the overwhelming majority of the population. And this struggle is going to require a level of mobilization and commitment beyond what happened in the past. Society is much more globalized today and that means struggle has to be more international, solidarity has to be across borders. That is coming too, but the question is, is it fast enough?

Let me give you another example closer to home for me – the North American Free Trade Agreement (NAFTA). To start with, NAFTA is misnamed. It certainly was not an agreement, least of all an agreement involving the general population of the three countries (Mexico, Canada and US). The population was strongly against it. So if it was an agreement, it was between somebody else and not the population of these countries. And it was not about free trade. It was about strengthening investor rights, which is quite different from free trade. In fact, at that time, about half of US exports to Mexico didn't even enter the Mexican economy. They are called "trade" by economists, because it happens to cross national boundaries. But if the Ford Motors company shifts components across the border to employ cheaper labor and evade environmental restrictions, and then sends them back across the border for adding more value, that is not trade in any meaningful sense of the word.

Coming back to NAFTA, the purpose was to raise investor rights. In order to get it through (the partners are democratic countries), they had to put in some side provisions about labor rights and environmental protection and so on. They are not meant seriously, but they are there. Right after NAFTA was enacted, General Electric and Honeywell, two big investors in Mexico, fired a good part of the labor force that was involved in union organizing. This is a radical violation of labor rights. Well for the first time ever, the American labor unions (which have had quite a reactionary leadership) stepped in and insisted that a case be brought before the US Labor Department. They instituted proceedings against these firms. Of course they lost: this is just cosmetic. But it happened, for the first time ever. A labor-based organization which until recently has been pretty marginal has been organizing pressures to demand elementary labor rights in the areas where US investments go. It's by now fairly successful. They have just compelled GAP, the big clothing manufacturers, to modify labor practices in Central America, where women are miserably exploited by textile manufacturers and the electronics industry. This may turn out to be cosmetic again (we don't know yet), but they have created a national scandal about it, and a lot of public pressure. GAP had to do something.

They may find a way around it, but those things are happening more and more. This is the kind of international, cross-country solidarity that can compete with transnationals.

But it has to go much further, to the extent of realizing that the whole system is fundamentally illegitimate. There is no justification for private corporations to exist. They would have horrified classical liberal opinion. You can already see that insofar as classical liberals (like Jefferson) still existed at the time when the corporations were rising, they were bitterly condemned. They came to power in the early part of this century and they have no right to that power, and certainly no right to the transnational power that they have. They have to be dismantled. That is going to take a big effort. But it's no bigger an effort than overthrowing feudalism. These things take long, committed, dedicated popular struggle. There are plenty of signs of it all over the place. But it is certainly not going to be simple. Anyone who wants a general strategy to do it by tomorrow had better look somewhere else. There is no new one, just the old strategies which worked in the past. There is no reason why they should not succeed again.

Question: *Those of us who were students forty years ago admired Nehru's socialism – which meant a state-controlled, or at least state-regulated, economy. Now we have moved consciously or unconsciously to a liberalized regime, where we are welcoming multinational companies. Even Jyoti Basu and Laloo Prasad Yadav, champions of the poorer sections, are welcoming this new regime. What is your advice for a country like ours? Is it just that we alternate between state control and multinationals, until some balance emerges?*

Chomsky: I don't presume to give advice to other people, and in particular, to other countries. They have their own complicated problems, which you have to work out yourself. Advising you about it would be ridiculous, as you know more about it than I do. However, there is something general going on. It was pointed out rather well by Bakunin about 150 years ago. He made one of the few significant predictions in the social sciences that's ever come true, and it ought to be studied for that reason alone. He predicted that within the rising industrial world there would be a new class of intelligentsia. They would fall into two categories. One category, he said, would try to use popular struggles to gain power for themselves and become a "red bureaucracy." It would create the most brutal tyrannies that humanity had ever seen, all in the name of the people (state socialism). The other category of intellectuals would recognize that instead of taking power to exploit popular struggles, it makes more sense to serve people who already have power. As he put it, they would "beat the people with the people's stick," in what we would now call state capitalist democracies. These would be the two major categories of intellectuals. For one of them, the way to beat the people is to take power and introduce something called socialism which means smashing every popular organization and keeping people under control. That's the red bureaucracy. The other category prefers to serve the powerful and beat the people with the people's stick, called democracy.

I think his prediction was right – those have been the two methods of beating the people. But do we need either of them? Why? If we look way back at the origins of modern democracy, if you look at the English revolution in the seventeenth century when you have the first modern democratic revolution, you find a pattern which has shown up again and again in every popular struggle I know of (and it goes further back in history). When you study in school about the English revolution, you learn that it was a conflict between King and Parliament as to who was going to take power, which is not false. But it is only partially true, because as in every other civil conflict that I've ever heard of, it wasn't just two parties contesting for power. It was three. There was also the general population, which didn't want either. As they put it in their own pamphlets, they wanted to be ruled by "countrymen like ourselves." They wanted to take control over their own institutions, without knights, gentlemen, parliaments, etc. They made some gains, and what there is of English democracy reflects these gains. The same happened with the American Revolution.

Are there alternatives to the two forms of tyranny? Sure there are – democratic control by ordinary people of every institution, whether it is industry, colleges, commerce, etc. There is no reason why these institutions can't be under popular control. It's true that this would not leave any place for the intellectuals. They wouldn't be able to take power as a red bureaucracy, or to serve private power and get the benefits that it offers for the service. Therefore intellectual opinion is overwhelmingly opposed to popular control, which makes good sense given their class interests. But there is no particular reason why anybody should accept this.

Question: *I think the whole debate is misplaced. Some people support the concentration of wealth in a few hands, others the concentration of rights. Both believe in concentration. The debate should shift from there, and the state should be called upon to eliminate injustice.*

Chomsky: The rights that are concentrated in the existing society relate primarily to the right to property. There are plenty of other rights, and they are important and have been won by popular struggle. For instance, freedom of speech is an extremely important one, which has been achieved in the US beyond any other country in the world. And it was achieved recently. It is written in the Bill of Rights, but that's meaningless. All sorts of things are written in the Constitution. Freedom of speech was actually achieved in the 1960s, even formally when the Supreme Court struck down the law of seditious libel – the law which protected the state against criminal assault by words. Just about every society has that in some form. England still has it, so does Canada – in fact everyone I know of. But it was finally struck down in the US, which means that state authorities are no longer protected from assault by words. The courts went on to achieve further libertarian standards, also unique to my knowledge, while allowing certain narrow departures from full protection of freedom of speech, which I think are legitimate, namely that speech ought to be protected up to incipient criminal action. For instance, if someone comes to a store with a gun and you tell him "shoot," that speech is not protected. But up to criminal action, freedom of speech exists and it's a very important right. Those kinds of rights are not concentrated – they are general rights to, say, freedom of speech. Everybody can use it. Now in fact, only a few people can use it, namely the people who have property, but that's because of property rights which allow other rights to be actually enjoyed by people who are privileged. It's no argument about other rights. It's an argument for getting rid of the concentration of power. So I don't see the conflict you described. Some rights ought to be general, and other rights that are concentrated, like property rights, ought to be eliminated so that all rights become general.

As to calling upon the state to eliminate injustice, I don't understand what that means. States are exactly the way Adam Smith described them, combinations of the rich and the government to oppress the poor. You don't call upon that combination to get rid of injustice, what you do is dismantle it. This doesn't mean tomorrow. What you want to do is to place power and authority, ability to make decisions, in the hands of popular groups. That doesn't mean calling on the state to eliminate injustice, it means getting enough power either through or over the state, or after the state is dismantled in anything remotely like its existing forms, so that people can eliminate injustice – like instituting freedom of speech. But you don't call on a power system to eliminate injustice – that's like calling on a corporation to be benevolent. It doesn't make sense.

Question: *There are of course many examples of organized resistance to global liberalization outside the US. But since your primary concern has been with the US, what are the possibilities for organized resistance within the US?*

Chomsky: I mentioned yesterday that, in all this talk of mass depoliticization in the US, there is one oversight – namely that there has been a lot of organization and politicization, though it's rarely studied. In fact, there has been a tremendous amount in the past thirty, thirty-five years, and that's quite important. What the elite calls "the crisis of democracy" is very real. There has been considerable change from the apathy and obedience of 1960 to much more activism today, and it shows up in all sorts of areas. It started in the 1960s, and took off in the 1970s and 1980s. The big popular movements that have made a lot of difference, like the feminist movement or the environmentalist movement or the solidarity movements, are movements of the 1970s and 1980s. There is little talk about them, because you are not supposed to let it be known that there is resistance. Remember, you're supposed to make people believe that everything is hopeless. But these movements take place, on an enormous scale. And they have led to major changes in the country; outside educated circles – which are mostly untouched for obvious reasons – the general population is simply very different.

The Vietnam War is a striking example. In 1962, J.F. Kennedy started sending the US Air Force to bomb South Vietnam. Before that, South Vietnam had been a standard Latin American-style terrorist state. The US had instituted a terror state there, which was slaughtering the population but couldn't control popular resistance, so the US had to move in directly. So the US Air Force started bombing, and Americans went into combat operations. And nobody batted an eyelash. You couldn't get two people together in a living room to talk about it. It's not that it was a secret. You could read in the *New York Times* about the bombing missions carried out by the US Air Force. But so what, we want to bomb another country, that's their problem. In fact, the operation was so widely supported, not only in the US but all over the world, including India, that people do not know that the US attacked South Vietnam. Ask your sophisticated friends when the US attacked South Vietnam, and very few will know what you are talking about, because the idea that the US was attacking South Vietnam was inconceivable to general opinion at that time. If the US wanted to attack another country, that's its prerogative. In the US this was unquestioned. And it remained unquestioned among elites. So among educated sectors, opposition to the war was always on "pragmatic" grounds. A noble cause, but costs too much, can't get away with it. The whole flak about McNamara's book was about that. He says it cost us too much. And then the whole debate was – did he go too far? Maybe it was right for him to say that? A total scandal. It doesn't matter how much it costs you. It matters how much it cost those several million people you killed. But that's not an issue among educated sectors. On the other hand, that's not true among the population. Since around the early 1970s, when polls started asking people about their attitude towards the Vietnam War, about seventy percent steadily said that the war is fundamentally wrong and immoral, not a mistake. That is the position which everyone holds on their own. Nobody says it, they've never heard it. The most that anyone who has got a good education can say is, the war was a mistake, but for seventy percent of the population it was not, it was "fundamentally wrong and immoral." That runs right through the Reagan years into the early 1990s. Those are big differences, compared with the situation in 1961, and they show up in everything else.

When Ronald Reagan came in 1980, he was trying to duplicate Kennedy, his model. I should say, when people talk about Reagan they have to remember that he was like the Queen of England – who opens Parliament with a message, but nobody cares that she understands it, it's a symbolic position. When Reagan came in, they tried to duplicate the Kennedy operations, this time in Central America where the same situation had developed: they had terror states which couldn't control the resistance any longer. It looked like the US would have to invade, just like in South Vietnam. In fact, they announced it. As soon as they came in, they duplicated what Kennedy did, but the reaction was very different from 1961: there was a public uprising. There were spontaneous demonstrations all over the place, many of them centered on church and solidarity organizations. In fact, there was so much resistance that they had to back off. They told the press, forget it, we didn't mean it seriously. Instead, they moved to clandestine terror. That's bad enough, a couple of hundred thousand people got slaughtered, and four countries were nearly destroyed. But B-52s were far worse. The difference between B-52s and clandestine terror doesn't look like a great advance, but it is. So the Central American terror of the 1980s was not direct aggression, and it wasn't like Vietnam, where they sent the American army to wipe the place out. It was clandestine terror, and resistance was far beyond the 1960s. I mean, not only was it much broader, but it was deeper, rooted in the population and right in the mainstream. The main resistance was coming from churches, people in the Southwest – many were culturally conservative. But it happened all over the place, and at a level that was far beyond not only the 1960s but anything in the history of western imperialism. Remember, thousands of well-to-do mainstream Americans went to Central America to do things like living in villages, on the assumption that a white face around might restrict the terror against these people. That has never happened in the history of imperialism. Nobody ever dreamed of going to live in a Vietnamese village to protect people against marauding soldiers in the 1960s.

There was another dramatic example in 1992. It was 500 years since the "liberation" of the hemisphere, and they counted on a big celebration. They couldn't do it, not because of the radicals, but because the population just would not tolerate it – treating the initiation of mass genocide as liberation of anything. So they had to back off. Had it been thirty years earlier, no doubt there would have been a great extravaganza. In fact, all this hysteria about political correctness developed right at that time, and I suspect this was the reason for it. Among educated elites there was a real outrage that the population would simply not accept this, and the reaction was hysteria about the left takeover, political correctness and all that.

Well, those are very substantial changes. The country is very different from what it was, a lot more civilized in many ways. On the other hand, it is also a lot more irrational and hysterical. There has been destruction of resistance, the reaction has been very powerful and effective, but it is still there. That's what conflicts are like; much is going on on both sides. The people in paramilitary organizations etc., they could very easily switch. They could be a mass base for fascism, or a popular base for very constructive developments. It's like Germany in the 1930s – it could have gone either way.

Question: *The business world, if not the poorer classes, knows it's all class war. Do you think that any non-violent resolution of this class war is possible? Secondly, you have been a persistent critic of both the capitalist world and socialist countries. Would you like to elaborate on the alternative system you propose and how to achieve it?*

Chomsky: No sane person wants violent change. Of course, pathological people may want violence, but not people in their right minds. You do want to see more freedom, justice and democracy, but not violence. So when does it get violent? Well, it becomes violent if people who have power refuse to respond to calls for justice and freedom, and use violence to protect their power. So the question becomes whether it is possible to expand the realm of freedom and justice without running into state terror and other forms of repressive violence. That is not in the hands of people who are trying to expand the realm of freedom and justice. Naturally, they will try to do it non-violently and hope that they can. Many times, it has been done. If you look at the history of Scandinavian social democracy, they got that way quite fast, from pretty reactionary systems, and it has been done non-violently. Sometimes it's done with violence, and sometimes without. Generally, resorting to violence has very negative consequences for everybody. So if it does happen, it's a regressive step. It depends on the response you get from people with power. If people with illegitimate power use violence to protect their power, yes, there will be violent conflict.

Regarding the second question, about what alternative society will look like, I think you can sketch it out at various levels of detail, but it's not a particularly wise move. We do not understand enough about complicated systems. Incidentally, that begins around the level of big molecules – from that level on, understanding tails off very fast. So there is no point trying to design complicated systems, like alternative societies, in any detail. You can talk about principles they should try to realize. And you can debate the principles they ought to follow, and think of ways of implementing them in particular places. I think there are reasonable principles, which have been discussed for centuries. For example, workers' control over industry – that's perfectly reasonable. There is no reason why industrial enterprises should not be under the control of working people and the communities in which they live.

How would you work that out? We can give all sorts of details. First, we can find examples which partially realize workers' control, and think of ways to modify them. And then, to an extent, market principles should be allowed to operate. I have friends who are very confident about it and have very strong beliefs. But I don't see how they know, how anybody can be smart enough to know, whether we can completely eliminate market principles or just allow them free reign. You can see the consequences of some of those extreme choices, they are pretty bad. But there's a big range where you have to experiment. Should you use market principles for shadow pricing – not affecting what gets to people but determining where demand is? Maybe. I don't see that there is a principled argument about that. You have to explore and see what happens when you try. You are talking about extremely complex and poorly understood mechanisms, namely human society. And here, I think, it makes sense to be conservative – to try changes and see what happens. If they work, fine. But hitting a system you don't understand with a monkey wrench and saying it will get better usually doesn't work well.

So we can talk quite reasonably about principles and explore ways to implement them. In concrete situations, where we have a specific problem to deal with, we can work out detailed tactics – but they might be quite different in the next situation, and I think these are just learning experiences. You try and hope to do better the next time.

Question: *How do you place the war with Iraq or, more generally, against Muslim fundamentalism? Do you see it as a popular struggle? Do you see it as a democratic movement or something of that kind?*

Chomsky: Well, some sort of "clash of civilizations" is supposed to be going on between the civilized West and uncivilized Muslim world – that's the new enemy. However, let's be a little careful. First of all, the US has absolutely nothing against religious fundamentalism. It's probably the most religious fundamentalist society in the world. I'm not exaggerating. If you look at fanatical religious belief, it's hard to find any country that has more of it than the US. Literally half of the population in the US (an educated country where people go to school) believes that the human species was created a couple of thousand years ago. I don't know what the figure is in Iran, but it's unlikely to be higher. People in the US have born-again experiences, religious cults, and so on – it's beyond belief. So the US has absolutely nothing against fundamentalism. Does it have anything against

Islamic fundamentalism? Again, certainly not. The most extreme Islamic fundamentalist state in the world, and another monstrosity, happens to be a great US ally – namely Saudi Arabia. Does the US have anything against Saudi Arabia? No, as long as they do their job, and their job is to make sure that the wealth of oil production goes to the West instead of the population of the region. As long as they do that job, they can be as fundamentalist as they like. Nobody cares.

So what the US is against is independence. If an Islamic fundamentalist state or movement happens to be independent, yes sure, they're against it. But they're just as much against the Catholic Church. The war in Central America in the last decade (in the 1980s) was primarily a war against the Church, the Catholic Church. If you think about it, it's kind of symbolic (but more than symbolic) that the decade of the eighties in Central America began with the murder of an Archbishop and ended with the murder of six leading Jesuit intellectuals – in both cases by elite forces trained and armed by the US. This went on right through the period, and a very substantial part of that war was in fact a war against the Church. Why? Well, the Church had shifted from its historical vocation of serving the rich, and a very impressive section of it sided with the poor. As an old atheist, this is odd for me to say, but I ended up staying in the Jesuit House in Nicaragua when I visited (at the invitation of the Jesuit university, incidentally). These were really marvelous and courageous people who undertook what they called "the preferential option for the poor," meaning the Church would work for the poor and not the rich. That called forth a war of terror and slaughter, not because there is a clash of civilizations between the US and the Catholic Church, but because they were just working for the wrong people. That's the background for the story of Islamic fundamentalism. The real issue is that efforts to extricate oneself from a global system of domination are unacceptable, whether they are Islamic or Christian or right-wing or left-wing or parliamentary.

So, what was going on in the Iraq war? First of all, Iraq was a secular state. Saddam Hussein was considered a great guy by the US. He was a major friend and ally. If he wanted to gas Kurds, and purge dissidents, and so on, that was his own problem, but it was certainly not going to stop the US. The US intervened directly in the Iran-Iraq war in order to make sure that Iraq won, as it did. In fact, that intervention turned really extreme towards the end of the war. If you recall, the US naval forces in the Persian Gulf intervened openly on the side of Iraq, and even carried out one of the major acts of terrorism. The U.S.S. Vincennes shot down an Iranian airliner in commercial Iranian airspace. Incidentally, this is no secret. There have already been two major articles in the *US Naval Institute Proceedings*, the official journal of the Navy Department, going through that incident in close detail and giving enough evidence to indicate that it was an act of state terrorism: they shot down the plane purposely and seem to have known what they were doing. That's the point at which Iran finally backed off. They realized that the United States is not going to stop. After that, Saddam Hussein remained a leading trading partner and ally, getting big credits from the US to purchase more agricultural goods, and so on, and everything was just fine until 2 August, 1990, when he made a mistake that a lot of dictators make. One of the dangers of being so dictatorial is that, because you are totally isolated from any interaction, you develop a completely distorted view of the world. So Saddam Hussein thought that he was free to go on and do anything he felt like. He completely misinterpreted some instructions that came from the State Department. I don't believe, as many people do, that the US instigated the war. I think that if you look back at those April Glaspie exchanges, and so on, what happened is that the US was telling Saddam Hussein, look, if you want to rectify the border with Kuwait and do something to raise oil prices, we're not going to make a fuss. And this was perfectly true, because the US did not care about any of those things. Saddam Hussein misinterpreted that to mean "take Kuwait." Well, that's not permitted.

It is not permitted, because of something that the intellectuals of the world have been very careful to conceal. If you look at the literature on the Iraq war, it's enormous, but one thing is missing from it – even in the scholarly studies – and that is a look at the declassified records. We have a rich declassified record of British and American planning documents that bear quite directly on this, and they're the first thing that any sane person would look at. These records are very interesting, they're about thirty years old, but they go through the relevant period, namely the late fifties, when Iraq broke out of the Anglo-American system of domination of oil, causing a huge uproar in Washington and London. The British Foreign Secretary flew to Washington: they had big consultations. We have records of those, and the records lay out the background for the Iran-Iraq war. It took considerable discipline for scholarship and journalism not to look at any of this stuff. When you look at it, what you find out is that they took crucial decisions. One decision was to grant nominal independence to

Kuwait. Kuwait had been a total colony, but they were worried that this nationalism from Iraq might spread to Kuwait, and the way to contain it was to grant them nominal independence. Kuwait would remain under British rule, but with various trappings of independence which would dampen the nationalist fervor.

They made various other plans, and one of them was that Britain reserved the right "ruthlessly to intervene" (that was the phrase they used) if anything happened to upset the order in Kuwait. Why Britain? Well, in the postwar international settlement the US took over the Middle East for itself, but Britain was considered our "lieutenant," as a high Kennedy advisor put it, adding that "the fashionable word is 'partner.'" The British prefer to hear the fashionable word, so they have various illusions about a "special relationship," but in fact it was our lieutenant. With all its history of knowing how to smash Third World people in the face, Britain would be a useful lieutenant. So Britain was allowed to take control of some of the smaller things like Kuwait. Kuwait has a lot of wealth, but it's not like Saudi Arabia. US took over the big stuff, so Saudi Arabia – that's ours. But Britain gets the small things like Kuwait, and that was quite important. If you look at the planning records, you see that both Britain and the US recognized that profits from Kuwait were critical to maintain sterling, and the British economy, and so on, just as the profits from Saudi Arabia and Gulf oil are critical for maintaining the US economy. It's not the oil that they care about so much, but the profits from it, and if anything happens to disrupt this arrangement Britain would ruthlessly intervene in Kuwait. The US reserved the right to intervene ruthlessly in the region if anything more happened. That's the basis for what went on. Something happened that was going to disrupt the arrangement, so they ruthlessly intervened, as they said they were going to do, and for exactly those reasons. That had nothing to do with any threat to the control of oil, nobody was going to change that, but it definitely had to do with a threat to the profits from oil.

There's something pretty striking about the history of oil. In fact, some economic historians have suggested it's the reason why the oil companies were never much interested in India. Oil development happens mostly in countries where you don't have to worry about the domestic population, so that they're not going to get the wealth from it. If you look at the prospects in India, the wealth may go to the people in India, which is just not worth it. On the other hand, the Persian Gulf region is fine in that respect. Profits have to go to the West, that's the arrangement. The West means the US and its lieutenant, primarily, and the big oil companies that are mostly American, though some are British, Dutch, and so on. That's the background.

Now as soon as he invaded Kuwait, Saddam Hussein realized that he had made a bad mistake. One of the things we know about this by now is that, within a couple of days, Iraq started offering to withdraw. But the US and England did not want Iraq to withdraw. In fact, what they called the "nightmare scenario" was that Iraq would withdraw and leave behind a kind of puppet regime, which would mean that the arrangements for control over the system would have changed. Notice that if Iraq had withdrawn and left behind a puppet regime, it would have done exactly what the US had just done in Panama a couple of months earlier – invaded, stuck in a puppet regime and withdrawn. But of course, that's the prerogative of power. It's fine if the US does it, but certainly not Iraq or anybody who disrupts an area that's so crucial to the health of the international economy, which means the wealth of the powerful in the West. That's like readjusting the arrangements for distribution of oil profits. Therefore, things were set up from that point on to make sure that there would be a war, that Iraq would not withdraw. Withdrawal offers were blocked, negotiations were blocked, the international press (including the European press) had to completely conceal this, and it did. There were a few leaks in the US, virtually none in Europe. Discipline was perfect, to my knowledge, except a couple of articles – I wrote one in the *Guardian*, and there were a couple of others, but virtually nothing on the Iraqi withdrawal offers and the refusal to accept them.

Finally, they got the war they wanted, and that established, as George Bush put it pretty frankly, that "what we say goes" and people ought to understand that. You don't step on the toes of real power. If you do, you get smashed. And that's going to continue. The reason why the sanctions are so severe is that you have to make an example. That's something any mafia don would understand perfectly well. Suppose that somebody from the mafia runs a particular neighborhood and gets protection money from the local storekeepers. Then some store-keeper refuses to pay protection money. First of all, you send in the goons to take the money. But you don't stop there; you have to make an example of it. So you beat him up or kill him, or kill his family, or something like that, so that others get the idea that this is not the way to behave. The same lesson applies in the international arena. That's the reason for the almost hysterical hatred of Cuba, Nicaragua, Vietnam – anybody who stands up and does anything wrong really has to be punished.

So that's the Iraq war. Not that Saddam Hussein is a nice guy. He is a murderous killer, but that's not the reason for the war. His crimes were mostly committed during the period when he was a great friend and ally. It's not the crimes that matter, and it was the same with Stalin, Hitler, and everyone else. If you look back at the records, Truman and Churchill had no objection to Stalin's crimes. In fact, they admired him. In internal discussions, they were defending him; they talked about him as a man of honor, and that sort of thing. The question is, will he subordinate his domain to western interests? If he does, he can rule any way he likes. If not, he is an enemy.

4. The Nationality Question in the Contemporary World*

This talk was arranged at short notice, rather spontaneously, and my feeling is that the best thing to do in this short session may be to devote most of the time to interchange and discussion. I'm sure you have lots of things in mind, and I would be happy to try to address the issues you are interested in. This is an extremely broad topic, and instead of my speaking about it, it would be more constructive for me to react to what you think is important. However, since I was asked to speak, I will start with a few general comments on this very broad issue.

The question I was asked to address is how imperialist forces have been repressing national struggles. Fine topic. There's another topic that could also be discussed, and I think should at least be brought into consideration. The topic is how nationalist struggles, when they succeed, suppress the populations that were mobilized to carry out these struggles. Because one striking feature of nationalist struggles, over the centuries, including this century, is that while they often present a liberatory face and use revolutionary rhetoric, they are generally rather conservative, even reactionary. Very often, a reactionary nationalism presents itself as revolutionary, and in a sense, it is so in the context of liberation from foreign oppression, but it is led by ideologies and leaders who themselves institute new forms of domination and authoritarianism. You don't have to look very far from your own experience to see that – simply look at the recent history of India. But that's repeated, over and over again. I have had close personal involvement with many Third World liberation struggles and domestic ones of a similar character, I have been deeply engaged with

---

* Informal talk at Shankar Lal Hall (Delhi University) on 14 January 1996.

http://dx.doi.org/10.11647/OBP.0050.04

them for many years, and I have rarely seen an exception to this. However radical and revolutionary the rhetoric may seem, it is usually a cover for new forms of repression and domination that take over once the national struggle ceases. That's another aspect of the whole question that should be borne in mind. A nationalist struggle may be entirely justified, but that does not mean that it is revolutionary, even if its rhetoric is revolutionary.

So there is one question, as to what extent nationalist struggles themselves are opening the way to new forms of repression of the general population. Putting that topic aside, another question is, how great powers (those who are in a position to manipulate and dominate the world order) use their power to repress efforts at liberation and independence, including nationalist struggles. So take the last half-century, when the United States has been a dominant force in the world, although the pattern goes way back. The US simply took over from England, France, Holland, and others, who had been doing the same thing for centuries. In this last half-century, the US has been a sort of guardian of the interests of the wealthy sector of the industrial world. It has been interested in suppressing any challenge to that system of domination and control. That means it has been opposed to nationalist struggles, and it doesn't matter what their political character is – they can be from what's called the left, or the right, or anywhere. The US will oppose them if they seek independence or autonomous development. The official phraseology is that they refuse to act in a way that is complementary to the needs of the industrial West, meaning the dominant elements in the industrial West. So if some radical revolutionary movement is willing to subordinate its interests, in political and economic development, in a fashion that will be complementary to the interests of the West, it's tolerable. On the other hand, if a parliamentary democracy, following all the proper rules, attempts to pursue a course of independent development, it will be crushed. That's the history of the past half-century, case after case. I can run through particular examples, but I think you must be familiar with them.

Let me turn to a related issue, namely how the dominant ideologies of intellectual classes (not only in the First World but also in the Third World) mask the repression of independence, and nationalist struggles, and create other illusions. There is a kind of consensus position about what is happening in the world today. It was expressed, for example, in a review of the world situation, on New Year's Day in the *New York Times*, by a respected commentator. Reviewing the world scene, he says something like this – with the end of the Cold War, it was broadly assumed that we would have new opportunities for entering a period of justice, freedom, and all sorts of wonderful things, and then it quickly became clear that this wasn't true, because of the savage ethnic conflicts that arose, mostly in the former communist world. It became clear that we are now in the era of resurgent nationalism, and there are now new challenges to the civilized West. So we are back in trouble again. Bright hopes for the future have been dashed. The consequence of this, and that's an accurate account of the international consensus, is that the civilized countries of the West must adopt a new position towards intervention. They must now consider the need for a new category of intervention, namely humanitarian intervention. That means radically revising the theoretical framework of international law and world order. I stress "theoretical," because it's never observed in practice. The core element of the framework of international law expressed in the United Nations Charter is that the use of force is excluded in international affairs, except in a very narrow category of cases, in particular, in self-defense against armed attack from another state. So if someone attacks you along the border, you're allowed to use force in self-defense, until the Security Council acts. That's it. Period. Apart from that, the use of force in international affairs is excluded, except under explicit Security Council authorization. Well, if you look at the past half-century, you'll see how well that law has been kept. But anyway, that's the theoretical framework. The picture now is that we have to revise the theoretical framework and accept the responsibility for humanitarian intervention on the part of the civilized powers, in reaction to this new period in which savage ethnic conflicts are arising, primarily in the former communist world. That's the consensus, and this was an accurate description of it.

This description raises some questions of fact and some questions of value. The questions of fact are very quickly answered. They include whether it is, in fact, true that there is a new period of savage ethnic conflict, particularly within the former communist world. The main question of value is, if that's true, does it authorize the self-defined civilized countries to institute humanitarian intervention to save the poor people of the world, the barbarians, from their mutual slaughter?

As I said, the factual questions are very quickly answered – namely, it's all total and utter nonsense. There are major changes in ethnic conflicts, but they don't have much to do with what's being discussed. The major change actually took place around fifty years ago. Ethnic and national conflicts actually go back to the origins of recorded history, there's nothing new about that. But there was a major change in 1945. Up until then, the worst ethnic conflicts in the world were internal to the industrial world itself. It was Europe that was the locus of most of the violence and destruction. Europe was very destructive in the rest of the world too, but what it was doing internally was much worse. So for centuries the French and Germans were dedicated to slaughtering one another, and so on, across every combination that you can find inside Europe. It goes back to the pre-imperial and pre-colonial period. It goes back a thousand years.

Well, that came to an end in 1945, and that's a big change in the history of ethnic conflict. You can be quite confident that there will be no further savage ethnic conflict internal to the industrial world. And it's not because of any spiritual transformation, or anything of that kind. It's simply that the means of destruction have become so extraordinary, that the next time Europeans try to slaughter one another it will mean the end of everyone. There can't be another war, because they have constructed such devastating means of mutual slaughter that another episode in this long history of ethnic conflict would lead to a cataclysmic end. It is for this reason that savage ethnic conflict among the resurgent nationalisms of the industrial world declined – in fact pretty well terminated. That is a major change in the history of ethnic conflict, but it's not much discussed, although it's by far the most dramatic change.

Within Europe, this led to two contrary developments of much interest. I won't go on about it, because that's not what you are interested in, but they are quite significant. One is a move towards federalism, and the other is a contrary move towards regionalism. Both of these are happening in Europe today. On the one hand, there is a general move towards a European Union – a kind of federal Europe with a good deal of centralization of power, particularly financial power in the Central Bank, which could become a major economic and political force in the world. On the other hand, there is also a striking increase in localized regionalism: a revival of local languages and traditions, separatism, devolution – a move towards what's sometimes called a Europe of the regions, in which the currently existing states will themselves break up. That's already happening to an extent in Spain, it may happen in England and there are tendencies in that direction in other parts of Europe. It is, in part, a reaction to the centralizing trend, which is suppressing national identities and boundaries in a broader union. So these two tendencies are developing sort of in parallel, and there is plenty of internal conflict. Take a country like Belgium. The internal conflicts within Belgium, religious and linguistic and so on, are very bitter, and if it was a poor country you would see mass slaughter there. In a rich country, these things are sublimated and modified into other forms, mainly for the reason I mentioned, that mass slaughter is far too dangerous. So that's Europe – big changes inside Europe.

What about the rest of the world? Has there been resurgent nationalism and savage ethnic conflict since the end of the Cold War? Not at all. If you take a look at ethnic conflicts around the world today, virtually none of them have to do with the end of the Cold War. There are a few, but almost all precede that. In fact, about the only ones that have any connection with the end of the Cold War are those that are internal to the former Soviet empire. Inside the former Soviet empire, you find some rise of ethnic and national conflict after the empire collapsed – in Chechnya, Azerbaijan, the Caucasus, Armenia, among other examples. But there is nothing very special about that. It's perfectly normal, in fact inevitable, that when a system of tyranny, oppression and domination collapses, there will be turmoil within what was formerly subdued and controlled. Every imperial system that has eroded, or withdrawn, or collapsed has been followed by such violence and conflict. You know what happened when the British Empire collapsed, here and everywhere else. The same happened with the French empire and Dutch empire. The end of empire typically opens up opportunities that had been subdued under imperial control, which often take the form of ethnic conflict and national rivalry. In contrast with the ends of the European empires, the end of the Soviet empire has been remarkably peaceful. There has been plenty of violence, but nothing there even begins to compare with the end of European empires in the past fifty years. I won't talk about England, France and Holland, which you know. But take the most recent European empire – just twenty years ago the Portuguese empire collapsed. This was one of the earliest empires, but one of the weaker ones. Its collapse instantly led to a huge outburst of ethnic conflict, violence, massacre and slaughter far exceeding anything that has followed the end of the Soviet empire. The Portuguese empire was both in Africa and in Southeast Asia, and in both places huge massacres instantly began.

In Africa, this took the form of South African-based attacks against Angola and Mozambique, designed to make sure that they would not separate themselves and follow an independent course. Angola and Mozambique were controlled by the Portuguese. Once the Portuguese empire collapsed, they started moving in an independent direction and South African-based attacks immediately began, backed by the US and England. The UN Commission on Africa made an estimate of what the damage had been, and they estimated that in the Reagan years alone (in 1980-88, during the period of so-called "constructive engagement") the US and UK-backed South African attacks in Angola and Mozambique caused over a million and a half deaths, and 60 billion US dollars in damage. That's a huge amount of destruction, and the sources of it are essentially the industrial West: Britain and the US, with some support from France, and other countries too, including some Third World countries operating through South Africa as the medium. Somehow, that's not supposed to count in the history of ethnic conflict, although it vastly exceeds anything that followed the end of the Russian empire. In Angola, it's still going on.

Well, that's Africa. What about East Asia? Exactly the same story. In Southeast Asia there was one Portuguese colony that immediately began to move towards independence – namely East Timor. It was instantly attacked by Indonesia, within days of the Portuguese withdrawal. And that is the worst slaughter since the Holocaust, relative to population, far exceeding any other. If you look at the per capita death rates in East Timor in the late 1970s, they were much higher than in any other country. Now, the terror has subsided somewhat, and during the last couple of years East Timor has been perhaps second to Liberia in terms of per capita death rate. That's still very high. Now, why doesn't that count? Well, the reason is that Indonesia was the proxy for the western powers in Southeast Asia, in the same sense as South Africa was in Africa. So the Indonesian attack on East Timor was decisively backed by the US, which provided most of the arms and diplomatic support, and later by England, which took over as the leading supporter. Other countries supported it also, including regional powers. You might have a look at India's role, it's not too pretty. This is the Southeast Asian analogue of what happened in Africa: huge massacres, far exceeding anything that's followed the end of the Cold War. But it doesn't count, and there's a simple reason for it, namely agency. In the case of the end of the Portuguese empire, the terror and destruction trace right back to western powers, and therefore, they are immune from discussion by respectable intellectuals. Incidentally, that includes respectable Third World intellectuals; I don't want to suggest that this is a western phenomenon. They do the dirty work, but that's because they have more power.

Now, let's take a look at the post-Cold War period – the period when this new era of ethnic conflicts is supposed to have emerged. Obviously, the list does not include any of these cases, because they happened earlier and have to do with the end of other empires. In the former Soviet empire, yes, there are some conflicts. I mentioned the cases; they are significant, but not enormous compared with the conflicts that arose at the end of other empires. The major ethnic conflict that occurred since the end of the Cold War has been Rwanda; that's by far the biggest massacre. But that has nothing to do with the end of the Cold War. That's been going on for twenty or thirty years, and it has to do with the end of the Belgian, and French, and British empires – they are all involved there. There was a big slaughter in Burundi twenty years ago, part of the same conflict, and there was another one this year. The European powers were involved in various complicated ways – mostly France, in this case. But again, that has nothing to do with end of the Cold War.

The conflict that has received most of the attention is in the former Yugoslavia. That's been very brutal, particularly in Bosnia, although nothing like the scale of any of the others. For example, with all its horrors, the conflict in Bosnia does not begin to compare with what happened in Angola in the same years. But that's where the focus is – on the former Yugoslavia and the Balkans. Here again, it has nothing to do with the end of the Cold War. The former Yugoslavia was a western, mostly US, client. The break-up of Yugoslavia and the conflicts that took place there have a good deal more to do with structural adjustment programs that were instituted in the 1980s, and their usual disruptive effects, than with anything related to the end of the Cold War. Since Yugoslavia broke up, the western powers and Russia have been maneuvering and trying to figure out how to reconstruct it in a way that will restore their own domination. Now, they don't have quite the same interests. Russia is not strong enough to be part of the game, but even the European Union and the US have a somewhat different picture of how Yugoslavia ought to be reconstructed. They both want to have control, so Germany would like to control it, and so does the US, and they have somewhat conflicting interests. But basically, they agreed for some time that the way to resolve the conflict would involve a partition of Bosnia between a Greater Croatia and a Greater Serbia, and then the question is who is going to control Greater Croatia and Greater Serbia. Well, the US (by far the stronger among the two contending powers) has apparently won that. The US waited until the conflict had sort of simmered down, with the two sides more or less balanced in military force and exhausted after plenty of mutual slaughter. At that point, the US moved in to separate the warring parties and to institute a plan, in effect a partition. They may call it something else, but it amounts to a partition between a Greater Croatia, which is already pretty much a US client, and a Greater Serbia which it is hoped will become a US client. If that works out, the US would have effectively restored the situation that existed before the break-up of Yugoslavia, with US dominance in the Balkans. And that's quite important for US strategic planning.

That part of southern Europe has always been regarded as the periphery of the Middle East. In fact, until the mid-1970s, Greece was actually within the Middle East section of the State Department. It wasn't even considered a part of Europe, and pretty much the same applies to the Balkans: it's part of the peripheral system surrounding the Middle East oil reserves, which is quite a system. It goes from the Portuguese Azores, where there are military bases, through southeastern Europe, Turkey, Israel, Pakistan (reconstructed as a part of this system), Diego Garcia in the Indian Ocean and off to naval bases in the Pacific. This global system is the base for possible intervention in the Middle East, to preserve US control over the world's major energy resources. Southeast Europe is a part of that system, and the US would like to reconstruct it as a kind of a base, and is hoping to do it right now. There is more to it than that. There's also a conflict, again, between Europe and the US on how to gain control over the restored Third World in the East. With the Cold War over, most of East Europe is being returned to its traditional Third World status, from which it attempted to escape. And the question is, who is going to dominate and control it? So there's the same kind of conflict between Europe and the US there as there was over Latin America and other places, and a base in the Balkans gives a certain leverage. So there's global planning behind all this.

There is no need to go further into this, the main point is that it has nothing to do with the end of the Cold War, and the same is true if you run through the other cases. As far as humanitarian intervention is concerned, let me just mention that the idea is not as new as has been claimed. It goes back at least 150 years, and its origins are interesting. The first discussion of humanitarian intervention that I know of is particularly interesting, because of the unusual integrity and intelligence of the person who was responsible for it, namely John Stuart Mill. It would be hard to find a person of such honesty and integrity in educated circles today. And he did write a paper on humanitarian intervention in 1859. If you change a few names, that paper says everything that is being said today, and it's kind of interesting to look at it.

The question that arose in 1859 was whether England should intervene in the conflicts in Europe, or follow the moral principles, which are now called international law, and say that you should not use force unless you are attacked. Mill opposed the dominant position in England which said, look, it's none of our business, we're not being attacked – let those guys fight it out. He opposed this on the grounds that England was not a normal country. It was a saintly and angelic power. It had no base motives, it was completely blameless, it wanted only equality and fraternity among people. In fact, he said England is so angelic that nobody can understand us; they attribute to us all sorts of base motives and don't see that we are just saintly creatures. Nevertheless, despite the fact that people are attributing to us these bad motives because they can't understand our magnificence, we should overcome our natural tendency to keep away from their struggles and should intervene. In particular, we have to understand that in conflicts between civilized nations and barbarians, the barbarians have no rights. Therefore, it is absurd to criticize the British for what they do in India or the French for what they do in Algeria, because that's arguing on the assumption that they are conflicts between civilized nations. They are not, they are conflicts between civilized nations and barbarians, where barbarians have no rights, and it's our duty as angels and Knights of the Round Table to intervene and solve the problems.

That was in 1859, and the timing is as interesting as the content. John Stuart Mill was a high official in the East India Company, as had been his father, the great liberal James Mill, and he certainly knew what was going on in India. You remember what was going on in India about that time, it was right after the suppression of the "Indian Mutiny" (as it's called in the West) with extreme barbarism, and the facts were very well known in England. There were parliamentary enquiries, and protests, and so on. Right after this episode of extraordinary barbarism, and with the horrendous second Opium War underway in China, a person who is almost unparalleled in integrity and understanding is capable of writing about how this saintly power has a right to intervene to defend civilization, and to defend the barbarians themselves from their uncivilized ways. Well, unfortunately, that's like what is happening today, except that it involves an even higher level of dishonesty. One can give other examples.

Going back to humanitarian intervention, this term is remarkable for its vacuity. You can't easily find examples of it in history – there may well be no such thing. When power systems use force, it is not for humanitarian purposes. If you can think of an exception to this, I would like to hear about it. Of course, every intervention is described as humanitarian, no matter what it is, including the Nazi conquests. But the fact of the matter is that these stories are untenable.

Since the end of the Cold War, the US has been involved in five military operations: Panama, Iraq, Haiti, Somalia and now Bosnia. I won't talk about it unless you're interested, but there is not a single case that can be described with a straight face as impelled by humanitarian motives. In each case, the usual narrow considerations of self-interested powers are the ones that motivate the intervention, despite the pretenses. In that respect, there has been no change. So the consensus picture seems to me to have no merit whatsoever. In fact, it is a tribute to the obedience of educated classes that this absurd story can be presented without ridicule. Again, I don't mean just the West here.

These are the kinds of illusions that mask the repression of independence and nationalist struggles. As I said, there is also a complementary question about the nature of nationalist struggles, and whether they are really liberation struggles, or struggles to institute new forms of oppression. That seems to be the sort of issue that should be considered when one thinks about the ethnic question in the contemporary world.

Question and Answer Session

Question: *What is nationalism, and how do we define a nation? Is language the criterion, or religion, or ethnicity? If so, then every few thousand people make up a nation. Please comment. Also, we face a dilemma because many people feel that this nation-state with its European historical basis is an outdated concept. At the same time, every nationalist struggle takes political guarantee for its identity. How do you resolve this dilemma?*

Chomsky: Well, the question about the criteria for nationhood has no answer in my opinion. The only way to decide whether some group of people deserves to be considered a nation is to ask them. If they say we're a nation, okay they're a nation. Beyond that, there are virtually no criteria. If you look at the things that are called nations, they are so in every imaginable fashion. So I don't think it's a meaningful question. People seek modes of identification and association with one another. They do it in all sorts of conflicting ways; they do it on the basis of friendship, religion, talking the same language, living near each other, whatever. Now, you also have transnational associations among people working in the same discipline, people who never met one another but are communicating all the time. There are all sorts of modes of mutual association. Some of them have been codified in things called nations, but it's not a meaningful concept. If people say they are a nation, and call for a right of self-determination, basically they have that right. Then you get into the question of conflicting rights, but that's a general problem. Any effort to assert legitimate rights will, quite commonly, run into the fact that it interferes with other legitimate rights. That's human life. That's the way relations among people work, and in a sort of civilized setting you try to work it out the best way you can.

Now, the nation-state was one form of answer to this question, and yes, it was a European invention. It emerged from centuries of terror, massacres, slaughter and devastation; you know the Hundred Years War, Thirty Years War, and so on. To impose the nation-state system in Europe was a brutal and bitter affair, which took hundreds of years and finally resolved itself in 1945, but only for the reason that I mentioned: the next effort to change the nation-state system would have led to total destruction. Therefore, the nation-state system was established. But it's a very unnatural system. You can see that from the savagery with which it was imposed, or sort of emerged. It is only very loosely related to people's natural interests. Therefore, it had to be imposed and redefined and reconstructed, and so on, by extreme violence. If you look at the history of the European conquest of most of the world, you find the same thing. It did leave a residue of nation-states, but they so radically cross-cut the natural forms of association that the imposition of nation-state systems has simply bred new and destructive forms of violence, which kind of reconstruct the internal history of Europe.

Is there a way out of this? Well, I think in the longer term the way out of it would be to try to erode the nation-state system altogether. I mentioned this move towards a Europe of the regions, devolution of the states into regional areas with some loose kind of federalism among them. It's probably a healthy development. To carry it out will not be a simple matter in Europe, and it will be even less simple in other parts of the world, but it's a pretty natural way for these questions to be ultimately resolved. However, that requires an erosion of other forms of domination and control, because this nation-state system is only one, remember. It's one that happens to have coalesced around another form of domination, national economies, which are themselves based on extreme forms of coercion and domination. Now, we have the systems of transnational corporate capitalism, which are state-based but quite global in character, and are developing their own forms of government at a transnational level. That's what the International Monetary Fund (IMF), World Bank and World Trade Organization (WTO) are, in effect. So all sorts of complex structures of hierarchy and authority, illegitimate authority, are interlinked, and in my opinion, they all ought to be dismantled. But that is going to require very extensive and committed popular struggle. Maybe at some point it ought to take the form of national liberation struggles, but if so, that should be done with question marks. And it's only one part of a much bigger story.

Question: *Do you think that there is a change in imperialism's strategy vis-à-vis the Third World states, in the context of the end of the Cold War and also of economic globalization?*

Chomsky: Well, you know, these categories I don't think are awfully helpful. Is there a new strategy for imperialism? Well, there is, there are new strategies reflecting new situations. I mean, the same principles operate, but there are new contingencies, so there are new strategies for dealing with them. On the other hand, the category of imperialism itself is pretty misleading, in my opinion. Take, say, the US, which is the dominant world power, so we could say that "imperialism" means anything the US is doing. However, US power is, to a very large extent, directed towards the US population. Is that imperialism? I don't know. It's what is happening. And there's nothing novel about the fact that a large part of the victims of US power is the population of the US itself. The same was true for the British Empire. If you do a sort of cost-benefit analysis of the British Empire, what Britain gained and lost from it, people have tried to do this and it sort of balances. The costs and benefits of empire appear to be pretty well balanced, a conclusion which seems reasonable.

If you ask whether America won or lost the Vietnam War, it's a meaningless question. Some in America gained, namely the ones who designed the policy, and some in America lost, namely the ones who did the work for them. That's a pretty common pattern. So when you ask what is the strategy of imperialism, this question presupposes that the nation-state is an entity that acts in world affairs, but that's not really true. The nation-state has to be looked at in terms of its internal structures of domination and control. When you look at those, you get quite a different picture, and that becomes even clearer when you move to a more globalized system of domination, as in the period of transnational corporations. For example, take a simple question, such as whether the United States is declining in its economic power in the world. It is very commonly said that US economic power is declining, relative to other countries. That's true, if you take the US to mean the geographical area, what is called the US on the map. If you look at the share of this geographical area in, say, manufacturing production, it is declining. On the other hand, if you define the US as a corporate power based in the US, if you take General Motors to be part of the US even when it operates in Poland or Mexico or whatever, and of course, that's the way it is thought of by the people who run the country, then it turns out that the US share in manufacturing production is not declining, it's probably increasing. It's just that these entities are distributing themselves, so as to gain cheaper labor and avoid environmental regulations, and so on, but the profits come back to the same sector in the US. The accountants for General Motors don't care whether exports are from Mexico or Michigan – it's the same thing. From that point of view, defining the US that way, its economic power is not declining, and that's a reasonable way to think about it.

Now, if we think about power systems as being class identified, then yes, their strategies change. One of the major developments in the contemporary world is that in the US and England, and increasingly in other industrial countries, the dominant classes (the ones who fundamentally run the place) are conducting a war against their own population. In fact, they are trying to turn around their societies into societies more or less on the Third World model. That's an important part of the new strategy of imperialism, which means that for a good part of the working population in the US, the country is moving towards Third World conditions. Being such a rich country, it's not going to look like India or Mexico, but the structures are more and more similar. That's the new strategy.

As far as running the international order is concerned, the use of violence is a last resort. You use it if you have to; if there are other techniques of control, you use them. And in the past twenty years or so, other techniques of control have come into operation. For instance, throughout the Third World, elite elements (including those who led nationalist struggles, I should say) are increasingly interested in associating themselves with international imperialism and serving as its agents, and instituting in their own countries policies that will benefit the privileged sectors of the world internationally and harm the mass of the population of the world internationally. That's called structural adjustment, which is being advocated by elite elements who will benefit from it themselves throughout much of the world, including India. That's the new strategy, and this new strategy has a lot of power behind it because of very substantial changes in the international economic order. These are new strategies designed for new contingencies, but I think that looking at it in terms of an imperial power dominating other countries misses a lot; for instance, it misses the role of Third World elites in implementing the same system for their own benefit.

Question: *World order seems to be a perennial obsession with the western rulers (from Alexander to the Ottoman, British and French empires), whereas in the East, this has not been the case. What accounts for this difference?*

Chomsky: The statement is just not true. If you look at the history of the East you get the Mongol invasions, the Mughals, and so on – it simply is not true. I mean, if you look at the last couple of hundred years, yes, the major power centers have come from a fringe of northwest Europe. That's a historical fact. But it certainly is not a fact about long-term world history, not by any means. The Persian Empire, for instance, did not come from the West. Every power that's existed has tried to extend its sway in one or the other form. There were periods of relative openness, for example, in East and Southeast Asia in the period before European colonialism (probably the only period in which something like a free trade regime actually was in place over substantial time). Not that it was pretty – it was very brutal and ugly, but it happened to be a relatively free trading area. Well, the Europeans broke into it and disrupted it and introduced new forms of violence, and so on, but the idea that the effort to control the world came from the West is not true. It's not sustained by a look at world history.

Question: *How does South Africa fit into your analysis, with the end of apartheid, and the fact that South Africans are no longer good facilitators for western capital?*

Chomsky: Well, South Africa is one case where a liberation struggle succeeded. It was very bitter and hard won, but it did have a level of success, and towards the end it didn't meet much opposition from the traditional rulers (the US and Britain, and even the South African elites – white elites – were sort of willing to go along with it). I think the reasons were several. One reason is that they didn't have much of an alternative except extreme forms of violence which would have been harmful to themselves. And secondly, because they assumed, possibly with justice (we'll see in the next few years), that the black leadership would assimilate itself to their system and become stratified in such a way that they would join. They would simply model the traditional system of domination with some of their own faces in the executive boardrooms. There is a likelihood that this will happen. There is a big internal struggle in the black community now in South Africa over this issue, and how it will work out you can't tell. But if it does happen, it will be very typical of nationalist struggles. Your own history is an example.

Question: *Lenin says that every state power is essentially an instrument of oppression of one class by another. Hence the need for evolution of state power per se. Do you agree with this?*

Chomsky: First of all, I wouldn't particularly call that Lenin's thesis; it's been everyone's thesis. For instance, it was stated very explicitly, in almost the same words, by Adam Smith long before Lenin, when he pointed out that laws and governments are combinations of the rich to oppress the poor.

Basically the same point with different words, and that's like a truism of history. That's what laws and governments are: instruments of oppression by which those who are able to control decision-making, for whatever reason (either they have more guns or they control the economy or whatever it may be), try to oppress everyone else. So it's not Lenin's thesis.

On the other hand, to mention Lenin is relevant, because he is a prime example of how it works. The vanguard party that took power in Russia in 1917 was dedicated to crushing the popular movements and turning them into what Lenin and Trotsky called a "labor army" that would serve the authoritarian leadership. That was their goal. That was the ideology, that is what Bolshevism was. It was a perfect example of a system of highly authoritarian domination masking itself in the rhetoric of popular struggle, and its real nature became clear instantly. The first thing that Lenin and Trotsky did was to crush every spontaneous working class or other organization or association that had developed in the pre-revolutionary period, from factory councils to Soviets and everything else. And they did it in a very principled way, the reason being their ideology. You can't accuse them of misleading anyone. It goes right back to the origin of Lenin's thought – that the mass of the population was too stupid and ignorant to do anything for themselves, so they have to be beaten into a better future by us, because we are the smart guys and know how to do it. That's what vanguard party theories are all about. Lenin was bitterly condemned for that by the mainstream of the Marxist movement, people like Rosa Luxemburg, Anton Pannekoek and others, even Trotsky, in the early part of the century. His thought was deeply anti-popular, anti-democratic and authoritarian, and as soon as he took power, he implemented it. So I think Leninism is a perfect example of the phenomenon that's being described. And when I was referring to the fact that nationalist struggles often mask their deeply reactionary and oppressive character in revolutionary rhetoric, this is one case that merits careful attention from that point of view.

If we look at the history of Lenin's thought, it's kind of interesting. In the early years it's very authoritarian. That's when Lenin was sharply condemned by people like Luxemburg and others, for developing a concept which would put the party as the ruler of the working class, the central committee as the ruler of the party, and the maximal leader as the ruler of the central committee – which is exactly what happened; it was a very good prediction from the mainstream Marxist movement. That's characteristic of Lenin's thought from his early days until 1917, and from 1918 on. If you look at the intermediate period of 1917, you get a different Lenin. His 1917 writings, like the April Theses and *State and Revolution*, have a kind of libertarian-left, anarchist character to them. That ended as soon as he took power. There are various ways of interpreting that. The natural way, I think, is that Lenin was a supreme tactician, and he realized that in order to gain popular support during a period of conflict he had better express the ideas of the masses, so he moved to the left. But as soon as he took power, he moved back to the right where he'd been all along. That's one interpretation, but I think a fair one, and not untypical of nationalist and revolutionary movements, I should say.

Question: *Going back to the US, what about ethnic conflicts, involving the Blacks, Hispanics, and so on? Will the melting pot eventually blow its lid off?*

Chomsky: These are not predictable things. I happened to be talking, at breakfast this morning, with an Indian meteorologist who was describing some of his work to me. He said that it is now well-accepted that it is theoretically impossible to predict tomorrow's weather. It's not just because of lack of data; there are principled reasons (having to do with non-linear systems and chaos theory) why you can't predict tomorrow's weather now. That's probably true. Similarly, it's impossible to predict the results of conflicts within very complex systems like human society. You can see the conflicts, try to understand them, and do something to resolve them, but these are not things you can predict.

These ethnic conflicts in the US are somewhat misinterpreted, usually because of a failure to recognize that race and class are closely correlated. Race is a funny notion; it doesn't have any real meaning. What's called race, you know, like Black, Hispanic, that sort of thing, versus White, is very closely related to class differences. And a lot of what are called racial conflicts are, in fact, class conflicts. In the US, this is masked by the fact that class is an illegitimate word. The only people who are allowed to use it are the business world. They use it all the time. They've always thought in terms of classes, crushing the masses, and so on. In fact, if you look at the business press, it looks like vulgar Marxist literature with all the values reversed. But outside the business world, one of the things you are taught when you become educated is that the United States is a classless society, everyone is middle class and there are no class conflicts. And US cultural domination in the world is such that most of the rest of the world adopts the same illusion.

But of course there are class conflicts in the US, as the business world knows very well, and they happen to be closely correlated with race conflicts. So when people talk about race, it's often a mask for class.

The commitment to denial of class struggle in the United States is so extreme that the census bureau does not even provide statistics related to class. It's one of the few countries where you can't find out what the mortality rate from heart disease is among working people, because there are no statistics for class. There are statistics for race, and people who have tried to work through the statistics have found significant differences, say, between Blacks and Whites in nutrition, mortality rates, and all these standard quality-of-life indices. But when you extract the class factor, you find that a large part of those differences are class differences. Within each class, there are also race differences, but they are small relative to the class differences, and that runs through everything. When people talk about the race and ethnic problem in the US, they are really talking fundamentally about the class problem, with racial and ethnic overtones to it that complicate it further. One can try to understand this, and try to do something about it, but predicting what will happen is impossible.

Question: *We know the problems, but do you have the solution? Also, you have been rightly critical of professional academics in the US and elsewhere. In Third World countries with a high proportion of illiterate people, what role do you envisage for the educated middle class?*

Chomsky: To start with, I'm skeptical about people knowing the problems. I don't think we know the problems; there are many illusions in the way we look at the problems – all of us. And I think it's a major task to extricate ourselves from systems of illusion and distortion, and to figure out what the problems are. I don't know of any area where that is not true. We are all victims of tremendous amounts of ideological domination; I really think the problems have to be thought through. So one part of the solution is to try to get a sensible understanding of what's going on. Now, that's not the kind of thing that intellectuals do in a seminar room. If you do that in a seminar room, you will end up with some other distortion having to do with the privilege of people of power, their right to rule and all that stuff.

You can predict that without any trouble at all. The way you learn what the problems are is by engaging yourself with people who are struggling.

That brings us to the question of the role of intellectuals. Well, it's not to talk to each other: that may be fun, but it's a waste of time. Their role, if people are illiterate, which is indeed a huge problem, is to help them overcome illiteracy. And first of all, what are intellectuals? I do not even know what the word means. Most of the people who have intellectual positions, let's say professors in universities, most of them do clerical work. They are called intellectuals for all sorts of reasons, but it's not because of the quality of the work they do. I have known taxi drivers who are more intellectual, so it simply doesn't correlate. Intellectuals are people who use their minds. Well, everybody uses their minds. Some people are in a position where they can't do it very much, because they are forced to kill themselves to survive. When you have to work fourteen hours a day to put food on the table for your children, you don't have much time to use your mind. If you're forced to perform repetitive tasks over and over again for a long time, you even lose your mind. Again, that's an insight that goes back to people like Adam Smith from classical liberalism. Which is why Adam Smith, contrary to what everyone is taught, opposed the division of labor. He said that in any civilized country the government is going to have to do something to block it, because it will turn people into creatures "as stupid and ignorant as it is possible for a human creature to be." So you can't be an intellectual if you have lost your mind by being forced into degrading tasks. Now, the people we call intellectuals are those who have a sufficient degree of privilege and authority to be able to use their minds if they feel like it. The job of those people is the same as that of anyone else who has privilege that he or she shouldn't have. The people in this hall, including myself, have privilege we shouldn't have. Well, we've got it, and there's no point pretending that we don't – we have education, and training, and too much money, and that sort of thing, and we should use it to try to help people who don't. That means learning from them, working with them, offering them what we can from our own resources. So that they can find out what the problems are, and help us find out what the problems are and work out common solutions. I have my own ideas as to what kinds of solutions there are, but people have to work out their own ideas.

5. Militarism, Democracy and People's Right to Information*

It is no great insight that we live in a world of conflict and confrontation, and that one crucial element of it is class war. Class war has many dimensions and complexities, but in recent years, the lines have been drawn very sharply. To oversimplify, but not too much, on the one side there are concentrated power centers, state and private, very closely linked. On the other side is much of the population, worldwide. Though one can't estimate with any precision, I think it is fair to guess that a large majority of the world population is unable to get involved in issues of broad significance, as this requires a degree of privilege. As for concentrated power centers, they pursue their war relentlessly. They never stop. They use every opportunity to press their agenda forward in the harshest possible way. In particular, they use crises, whether it's an earthquake, or a war, or September 11th and its aftermath. And in such circumstances, you can expect, and you discover, that they exploit the atmosphere of fear and anguish. They hope that their popular adversary will be distracted, focus attention elsewhere, and be frightened, while they continue to pursue their programs without any pause – in fact intensifying them, using the window of opportunity. And that's what is happening right now.

The adversary should, of course, refuse to accept this cynical framework. It should focus its efforts, also relentlessly, on the primary issues, which remain as they were before the latest crisis. The issues include the threat of militarism, which is indeed a threat to the survival of the species at this point, and a far-reaching assault against democracy and freedom, which has been part of the core of the neoliberal program for the past twenty, twenty-five years.

---

* Lecture delivered at the Delhi School of Economics on 5 November 2001, at the invitation of the National Campaign for the People's Right to Information.

http://dx.doi.org/10.11647/OBP.0050.05

Well, those are the things I'd like to talk about. Everything, of course, is open for later discussion, so don't feel constrained by that. But I can't really bring myself to turn to those topics without at least a word on the immense human tragedy that is unfolding before us right now. This tragedy is being planned and implemented very consciously by the United States and its allies since September 11th. The High Commissioner for Human Rights of the United Nations, Mary Robinson, was not exaggerating when she pleaded with the United States to stop the bombing of Afghanistan and warned that if it continued there could be a Rwanda-style slaughter. In fact, she might have been underestimating. According to US estimates, the number of people at risk of starvation, which was about 5 million, has increased by fifty percent since the bombing started. That's 2.5 million people who are being pushed right across the border of death from starvation. Mary Robinson's appeal was of course rebuffed. It was also unrecorded. Literally, it received three scattered sentences in the entire US press. Other appeals from senior UN officials, aid agencies and others were not even mentioned.

On September 16th, that's just five days after the terrorist attacks in New York and Washington, the US demanded of Pakistan that it terminate food supplies to Afghanistan. The country has been on a kind of a lifeline. And as one aid worker said afterwards, we've just cut the lifeline. The decision on September 16th to cut food supplies was a conscious, determined decision to starve several million people to death. Again, there was no reaction. The next day, as it happens, I was on national radio and television around Europe. No one was aware of this decision or could think of a single reaction to it in their own country. There was no reaction in the United States. So apparently it's considered entirely normal for western civilization to make a decision to kill 2.5 million people within a few months. And that shouldn't surprise anyone who is familiar with history. It *is* in fact normal, which is why there is no reaction to the silent genocide that may be under way.

Already before the bombing, the UN Food and Agriculture Organization (FAO) had warned that the threat of bombing had driven out the aid agencies, and driven people out of the cities into the countryside, in fear and desperation, and that a humanitarian catastrophe was taking place. After the bombings began, the Food and Agriculture Organization further reported that about eighty percent of the crop plantings had been disrupted, which means an even more severe famine for the next spring. The bombing itself has turned major cities into ghost towns. About seventy percent of the population has fled. As in other cases, like Iraq and Serbia, the bombing is directed against power stations, electrical supplies, water supplies, sewage systems, and so on. That's a form of biological warfare. That's exactly what it means to do this in an urban area. The population either flees to the borders, which are mostly closed, or to the countryside, where they are heading into the most heavily mined areas in the world. Even in normal times, the mines cause ten to twenty deaths or injuries every day, often among children. Now the casualties are increasing sharply. One reason is that the UN has been compelled to terminate its mine-clearing operations. Another reason is that the mines are now superseded by much more lethal weapons, namely the cluster bombs dropped by the US. These are anti-personnel weapons, which are designed to murder people. They don't affect tanks or buildings or anything like that. They are little things that a child will pick up or a farmer will hit with a hoe, and then they explode and send flashes that tear them to shreds. And they're extremely hard to dismantle. Some areas where they've been used in the past – like Vietnam and Laos, in what was then the heaviest bombing in history, in an isolated peasant society – are still littered with millions of cluster bombs, and hundreds or thousands of people are killed there every year. The manufacturer says, twenty to thirty percent of them don't explode, which can mean only one of two things: either incredibly incompetent quality control or else a purposeful concern to murder civilians. You can form your own view.

All this is happening essentially without comment, because in a way it's kind of normal, that's what the West has been doing to the rest of the world for hundreds of years. But the millennium begins with two monstrous atrocities: the terrible terrorist crime of September 11th, and an even worse atrocity that's following it, namely a purposeful, conscious program of mass murder, which may have excruciating dimensions. And while this is regrettably normal business in Europe and its offshoots, it's kind of remarkable to see that a country like India, which has been subjected to this torture for hundreds of years and might be expected to have some appreciation of what it means, is nevertheless enthusiastically joining the bandwagon.

These accumulating horrors bear very directly on the question of people's right to information. It's extremely important to ensure that that right is denied. So the facts I have just mentioned, though not really controversial, are almost totally unknown in the United States. Not one person in a million is aware of them. And there is a good reason for that: if people did have the slightest idea of what is being done in their names, there would be mass protests and policies would have to change. The United States is a very free country, it's uniquely free – I think, the freest country in the world – with regards to the right to information. And the task of suppression of that right is not undertaken by the state. The state may try now and then, but it is pretty ineffectual. The task of depriving the population of information is the solemn duty of the intellectuals, of the educated classes. It is what you're trained for when you go to a good university. Ensuring that the right to information is denied is also the task of the free press. That's why facts like these remain unknown. You can't carry out a mass genocide if the population is aware of what is being done. And when these controls break down, you do get strong popular reactions. Well, we're now living through this, it's not the first case by any means; we're living through an illustration which is so shocking that words fail, at least my words. It's not novel, we should be aware of that, and nor is it restricted to the United States and Europe. It goes back through history, as does the role of the priesthood, either religious or – in modern days – secular priesthood.

Well, with these hopelessly inadequate words on a crime that we should be working day and night to try to bring to a quick end, let's turn to the topics at hand. Perhaps the best way to approach them is within the framework of this fashionable notion of globalization. But before doing that, it's important to clarify what globalization means. Like most terms of political discourse, this one has a literal meaning and a propagandistic meaning. In the literal sense, globalization just means international integration, mostly economic integration. And that's neither good nor bad in itself; just as trade is neither good nor bad in itself. It depends on what the human consequences are. It can be done in many different ways. That's the general meaning. The propagandistic meaning of globalization, which is used and enforced by concentrated power, refers to a very specific form of international integration: one which has been implemented with considerable intensity in the past twenty-five years or so, and which is designed in the interests of private concentrations of power. The interests of others are incidental. They may gain, they may lose; it doesn't really matter. The fact of the matter is that most of them lose, but that's just an incidental consequence.

So that's the propagandistic sense of globalization. And with that ridiculous terminology in place, the great mass of the people of the world who object can be labelled as "anti-globalization." They must be primitivists who want to go back to the Stone Age and are resisting inevitable forces. They want to harm the poor. I'm sure you're familiar with these and other terms of abuse. Opponents of globalization, I think, make a very great mistake if they accept this framework of power and agree to call themselves "anti-globalization." No one sensible is opposed to international integration, least of all the left. The left has been animated by a vision of globalization since its origins, certainly its modern origins. The whole vision of the left has been one of internationalism, of international solidarity and cooperation. And there have been very important strides in this direction, many achievements in recent years. We should be committed to that. We should be committed to far-reaching globalization, but designed to improve the lives and opportunities of people, of the people of the world, and the people of future generations. That's a task that cannot be put off. These are not empty words. The possibilities for moving forward are very real; they are illustrated in many ways. By now, the annual meetings at Porto Alegre in Brazil are important expressions of this. They bring together a very broad international constituency: Brazilian workers, the landless workers' movement, North American unionists, environmentalists, peasant movements, women's rights activists, many others. A very wide range of people who in the past have had nothing much to do with one another. They went on separate paths, but are now moving forward together in impressive ways, thanks to a constructive form of globalization that we ought to support, and this is part of the traditional vision of the left. Their actions are in part defensive, defending themselves against attack, but in part quite constructive, working on ways to dismantle concentrated power systems to extend popular control worldwide. That's the form of globalization that should be pursued, at least by people who want to create a world in which a decent person would want to live.

The specific form of globalization that is being officially pursued is quite different. That's called, as you know, neoliberal. That term, too, is highly misleading. What it refers to is not new, and by no means liberal. That should be obvious in India, more than any other place. The whole history of India, for the last several hundred years, is a classic example of how liberalism can be distorted into an instrument of power and destruction. And the current version of neoliberalism is similar to what destroyed India, based on a combination of imposed liberalization on India alongside of massive state power and protectionism in the imperial power. The current version of neoliberalism also adopts the traditional double-edged doctrine of liberalism and free trade. This doctrine says, free trade is fine for you, so that I can demolish you. But for myself, I'm going to insist on state protection and other devices to avoid the costs of market discipline, except when the playing field is levelled, to use the standard term, which means when it's tilted so sharply in my favor that I am confident that I can win. In that case, I'll favor free trade.

The fact that the new doctrines adapt the traditional ones to current circumstances should not be very surprising. Actually, it's exactly what you would expect if you look at the designers. The designers are the richest and most powerful states, the international financial institutions that follow their directives, and an array of huge corporations which are tending towards oligopoly and anti-market principles in most sectors of the economy. These mega-corporations rely heavily on the state sector, which is very dynamic in the rich and powerful countries like the United States. They rely on the state sector to socialize costs and risks, to privatize profits, and to maintain the dynamism of the economy. That's the real world economy. It's quite different from what you study in an economics class.

The designers of the system modestly call themselves the "international community." But maybe a more appropriate term is that used by the world's leading business journal, London's *Financial Times*, which described them as "the masters of the universe." That was last January when they were meeting in Davos, Switzerland, to organize the world. Maybe that was intended as ironic, I don't know, but it's accurate. The masters of the universe profess to be admirers of Adam Smith, so you might expect them to abide by his description of their behavior, although he only called them "masters of mankind" – but that was before the space age, remember. Smith was referring to the "principal architects of policy" in England, merchants and manufacturers, who, as he put it, attended to their own interests carefully and made sure that they were satisfied, no matter how grievous the effects on others, including the people of England, but, incidentally, primarily India. He wrote with particular anger about the savagery of the English in India and especially Bengal. He stated that the principal architects followed what he called "the vile maxim of the masters of mankind," namely all for ourselves and nothing for anyone else. That's an accurate description of the masters of today's universe, who follow this model, not noticing that Smith was denouncing them, not providing a model for them.

In subsequent developments over time that would have appalled Adam Smith or any other classical liberal, these huge concentrations of power have emerged, which are basically tyrannies. The courts have assigned to them the rights of persons, immortal persons, and proceeded to attribute the rights of persons to corporate management. That's true in the United States, and I think elsewhere. In recent agreements, mislabeled trade agreements, the rights of these private tyrannies have gone way beyond the rights of persons. For example, General Motors can now demand and receive, under WTO rules, what's called "national treatment" in Mexico. They have to be treated as a national company. On the other hand, if a Mexican of flesh and blood tried to obtain national treatment in New York, he wouldn't last very long, if he could even make it that far. So the corporate entities, the immortal persons, now have rights far beyond human beings. They're a strange sort of person, apart from their massive scale and immortality. The recent agreements give them even further rights, which are being explored and implemented for corporate entities to undermine regulatory legislation in the United States, Canada, and other countries, on the grounds that these regulations are what is called "tantamount to expropriation." To take a recent case that was won, a US corporation wanted to store toxic wastes somewhere in Mexico. The people of Mexico objected, they didn't want toxic waste stored there, and they turned the area into a national park. The corporation, Metalclad, charged Mexico with actions that are "tantamount to expropriation," because they infringe on future profits of the corporation. And they won. They won in a NAFTA hearing and finally in a judicial hearing, and the judicial hearing was correct, because the NAFTA rules do permit that. This is under an imaginative doctrine called "regulatory takings." Any regulation is a taking of people's rights, meaning corporate rights, because it might reduce their future profits. Well, those are no rights that a person of flesh and blood can think of, but they apply to these totalitarian institutions that dominate the international system, the masters of the universe.

All this is simply one part of a very dedicated assault against popular sovereignty, which means democracy. This assault is expected to become more severe. In the western hemisphere, there are now plans for a Free Trade Area of the Americas. There was a summit of the countries of the western hemisphere, last April in Quebec, with plenty of disruption and violent protest. The plans are being kept secret. Nobody knows in any detail what the plans are for the Free Trade Area of the Americas, and it's important to ensure that they remain secret, because if they become public, opposition will be overwhelming. I'll come back to that interesting exercise in thought control in a free society.

Well, the crucial point is that the public has to be kept unaware. That's been true all along. NAFTA, the North American Free Trade Agreement, is now seven years old. To this day, the press has refused to publish the official position of the labor movement on the form that NAFTA should take. That goes back to 1992, almost ten years. The press has also refused to publish the analysis of NAFTA that was done by Congress' own research bureau, the Office of Technology Assessment, which is very much like that of the labor movement. The reason is that this analysis was critical of the form of international integration that was being imposed by the masters of the universe, and therefore the public better not know about it. Because if the public knew about it, the already majority opposition to NAFTA would grow substantially, as people came to understand that their own individual criticisms were in fact well-grounded in substantial institutions. A central part of the neoliberal reforms is to reduce the threat of democracy – in this and other ways.

I mentioned that the one participant in the class war always exploits every opportunity to institute harsh and regressive measures, with unrelenting intensity. That's happening right now. The victims are told that they have to be subdued and acquiescent out of patriotism. On the other hand, patriotism does not prevent the masters of the universe from using the opportunity to give new tax breaks to Enron, to mention a company you've heard of around here; to increase the military budget substantially while nobody is looking; even to institute what's called "fast-track legislation." It's interesting how the US trade representative Robert Zoellick announced, immediately after the September 11th attacks, that the best way to combat terrorism is to implement fast-track legislation. What is fast-track legislation? Well, it's legislation that literally turns the United States into the Kremlin under Stalin. The legislation grants the executive branch the right to negotiate international treaties in secret, with no Congressional participation and, of course, no public knowledge. And then Congress is allowed to say yes. That's the degree of public participation. So that's fast-track legislation. It's often called "free trade legislation," and that's not entirely untrue. You couldn't pass legislation that's mislabeled free trade if the public had any participation. So it has to be done Kremlin-style. Undoubtedly, Osama bin Laden will just be shaking in his boots if this legislation is passed. It's such an obvious attack against international terrorism. Well, that's the kind of thing that it makes sense to press through when you have a window of opportunity, and the general public can be induced to keep quiet out of so-called patriotism or fear or whatever.

All this does raise a question. It's been very obvious over the past years that opposition to corporate-led globalization is overwhelming across the world. That's been particularly dramatic in the South, where the main opposition developed. It later spread to the North, where it becomes harder to ignore – so when it reaches Seattle, you can't pretend it's not happening. This raises the question of why there is such massive public opposition in the United States, in England, everywhere else. It seems paradoxical because globalization, so-called, as we are told every day, has led to enormous prosperity. In the United States particularly, it has led to what's called a fairy-tale economy. Just to give one quote from the extreme left of the admissible spectrum, Anthony Lewis, writing last March in the *New York Times*, said that globalization has created the greatest economic boom in American history, in fact the greatest economic boom in world history. So, why are people opposed? Well, it's admitted that the process has some flaws. Not everyone is participating in the glorious experience, and since we're good-hearted people, you know, especially the left, we have to be concerned about this. We have to worry about these people who lack the skills to join us in participating in the greatest economic boom in world history. And that also poses a dilemma. Why is it that this enormous prosperity that's developing and leading to fairy-tale economies is also leading to inequality? What do we do about that? Well, that picture is so conventional that it takes a bit of a wrench to recognize that it is entirely false in every respect, except one. The one true statement is about rising inequality. Everything else is totally and uncontroversially false. During the economic boom in the United States in the nineties, per-capita economic growth was about the same as in Europe. It was much less than in the pre-globalization period, the period before the neoliberal reforms of the 1970s. It was vastly less than during World War II, which saw the greatest economic boom in American history under a semi-command economy. So the question is how can the conventional picture be so different from the absolutely uncontroversial facts? Well, the answer is very simple, and you know it very well in India. A small sector of the society has in fact benefited enormously. And that sector happens to include the people who tell everybody else the wonderful news. And they're not being dishonest. You can't accuse them of dishonesty. They have every reason to believe what they are saying. They can read it every day in the journals for which they write. Furthermore, it's exactly what they see around them. You go to an elegant restaurant or the Faculty club, or the editorial office, or wherever you hang out. That's what you see. People who are enjoying a fairy-tale economy. So there's no reason to doubt it. It's only the world that's somehow different, and who knows about that.

Let's take a quick look at the historical record on this. Economic integration – globalization in the neutral sense – increased very rapidly in the half-century or so before World War I. It stagnated between the two world wars. Then it began to pick up again after World War II. By now, it's reached a level which is more or less comparable to about a century ago in gross measures, but only gross measures. If you look at the finer structure, it's quite different in interesting respects. Prior to World War I, there was much more international integration at the level of people. That is, movement of people was much freer, and those of you who care about free trade may recall that "free circulation of labor" is a foundation of free trade, according to old-fashioned radicals like Adam Smith. So the movement of people is cut back a lot by state regulation. On the other hand, the free flow of short-term speculative capital has risen to astronomical levels, way beyond anything in the past. This contrast reflects the central features of contemporary globalization. It expresses the relative value of people and capital. Capital has priority and people are incidental. Note that this is exactly the opposite of classical economics, from Adam Smith to David Ricardo. Both insisted that people should be mobile, and capital should be immobile. Everyone's heard of Adam Smith's invisible hand, and how wonderful it is. But apparently, not many people have read the one passage in *The Wealth of Nations* where he uses the phrase. It appears once, and it appears in the course of an argument against capital mobility and imports – against neoliberalism. He argues that the invisible hand will prevent this disaster from happening. Somehow, this passage has been suppressed. There are other interesting differences between economic integration in these two periods; I'll come back to some of them.

There is also a more technical definition of globalization, whereby globalization is measured by convergence to a single market, to a single price and wage around the world. Well, that's exactly the opposite of what has happened. Globalization has gone in exactly the opposite direction, creating enormous inequality. So there's a theory on one side, and there's a real world on the other side. And that's expected to continue. The US Intelligence Services recently put out a document, a projection for the next fifteen years, with the cooperation of academic specialists in the business world. The document describes various possible scenarios for what's ahead. The most optimistic scenario, it says, is that globalization will continue "on course," I'm quoting now, "its evolution will be rocky, marked by chronic financial volatility and a widening economic divide." That means there'll be less globalization in the technical sense, but more globalization in the doctrinally-approved sense – wealth for the rich. Financial volatility, of course, means slower growth. So the best scenario, best possible scenario is even slower growth and much less globalization in the technical sense, meaning more globalization in the sense that they like.

Military planners adopt exactly the same assumptions. There's now a vast expansion of armaments going on, primarily in the United States. Since September 11th, it's been escalated, using the window of opportunity. And there's a reason. If you look at the planning documents of the past years, they make the same prediction: they predict, in contrast with economic theory, but consistent with reality, that globalization is going to lead to an increasing divide between a small number of haves and a large number of have-nots. And that raises a problem, a problem that has the technical name "enforcing stability." Here stability means, "you do what I tell you or else," and it's hard to enforce stability when you have a growing mass of have-nots who are disruptive and unpleasant. Accordingly, it's necessary to have a huge expansion of the military.

The United States is already far in the lead in conventional forces and weapons of mass destruction. Actually, it outspends the next fifteen countries. But that's not enough; it has to move to a new frontier which hasn't been militarized yet – space. That requires a violation of the Outer Space Treaty of 1967, which has been observed so far. It has prevented the militarization of space. The United Nations is aware of this, in fact the world is aware of this, so there's been a reaffirmation of the Outer Space Treaty for the last few years, passed almost unanimously with two abstentions: the United States and Israel (and probably India next year, which is keen to join the race to destruction, for reasons you can explain to me). The UN Conference on Disarmament has been stalled all year for the same reason

– it is trying to put a restriction on the militarization of space, and the US blocks this. All this goes unreported in the American press, for the usual reason. It's not wise to allow citizens to know of plans that put the survival of the species at serious risk. Extending the arms race to space is, in fact, the core program, and it has been for years – it's not just Bush. "Race" is not a very good term since the United States is racing alone for the moment, though there are others eager to join – India, for example, has won a lot of respect from hawks and jingoists in the United States for its enthusiasm about this, which is in fact unique.

The plans to cross the last frontier to militarization of space are sometimes disguised as "missile defense," ballistic missile defense. Anybody should understand that when you hear the word "defense," you think "offence." Any offensive action is always called defense, and it's pretty straight in this case. One of the goals of militarization of space is to place offensive weapons, destructive offensive weapons, in space. And the goal is very frankly expressed. It takes real discipline for the educated classes to keep people from knowing this. It's all in public documents, very frank and clear for years, you can even read them on the internet. The goal, as the US Space Command documents explain, is to obtain global dominance, "hegemony" as they call it, and the purpose is (I'm quoting) "to protect US interests and investments." They also give a history. They say that in the past, countries constructed armies and navies to protect and enhance commercial interests, but now there's a new frontier we can cross. We can take the next step in protecting and enhancing commercial interests and investment, namely the militarization of space.

Now, this is known to be extremely threatening. There's no question about this, because of the predicted reaction among potential adversaries, or for that matter because of what are called "normal accidents" in the technical literature. A normal accident is the kind of accident you know is going to take place in any complicated system, you just can't tell when. And what's being planned are systems of great complexity, weapons of destructive power comparable to nuclear weapons, laser weapons powered by nuclear power, which itself is extremely dangerous in space. These weapons are to be on a hair-trigger alert, with automated launch-on-warning systems, because you can't take any chances. If anyone starts shooting down your satellites, your system is gone. So you have automated systems of massive destructive power, which are likely to undergo normal accidents, and maybe wipe everyone out. This could be stopped, nobody doubts that it could be stopped, namely by treaty. But to stop it would be inconsistent with the prevailing value system. The prevailing value system is that hegemony is much more important than survival. And that's not new, in fact, it's the history of hundreds of years, but the change now is that the stakes are far, far greater.

Back to globalization, the crucial point here is that these decisions are motivated by the expectations for globalization. Globalization is expected to lead to a widening divide, meaning failure in the technical sense but success in the doctrinal sense, and that requires weapons of mass destruction targeting the growing number of have-nots that globalization is expected to produce, and severely raising the threat to survival. And it's all very rational, within the framework of a kind of lunatic system of institutions.

Well, let's return to "the greatest economic boom in American and world history." Remember that this was written before the crash, before the fiscal bubble crashed early this year, at a time when things really looked fantastic. Since World War II, there have been two sharply different phases in the world economy. There was a phase called the Bretton Woods period, from shortly after the Second World War to the early 1970s, and then the neoliberal phase which followed it, when the Bretton Woods regulations were broken down. The Bretton Woods system in the first period was based on regulation of capital flows, so states could regulate outflows and inflows of capital, and currencies were fixed pretty closely to one another. That was terminated in the seventies. Of these two periods, it's the second that's called "globalization," though, in fact, international integration proceeded more quickly during the first period. But remember, this is a propagandistic sense of the term globalization, interpreted as neoliberal globalization. These two phases are quite different. Economists commonly refer to the first phase, the Bretton Woods phase, as a golden age, and to the second phase, the neoliberal phase, as a leaden age. And if you look at standard macroeconomic indicators, that's exactly what you find. They all decline considerably during the globalization period. That's true of the rate of growth of the economy, of productivity growth, of capital investment. In fact, even trade – the growth of trade has declined during the globalization period. The interest rates have gone way up because countries, especially in the South, have to protect their currencies from attack. That slows down growth, increases financial volatility, and has many other harmful consequences.

Let's come back to that profound dilemma everyone's worried about: what are we going to do about the fact that globalization has created this enormous prosperity, but also led to rising inequality? Well, there's no dilemma. There's nothing to answer. There's no prosperity. In fact, globalization has reduced prosperity, even by standard macroeconomic measures, which are highly ideological, but even by those. And it's not controversial. Many economists attribute the severe economic deterioration during the globalization period to the liberalization of capital flows (Eatwell and Taylor, to mention two prominent ones). You can debate that. So little is understood about the international economy that the causal relations are hard to establish. But the correlation is pretty clear, down to fine detail in fact.

What is even clearer is that financial liberalization does lead to an attack on democracy. That's not controversial. In fact, that was the primary reason why the framers of the Bretton Woods agreement, back in the 1940s, insisted on capital controls and regulation of currencies. They understood that this would provide some space within which countries could pursue social democratic policies, welfare state policies, without being overwhelmed by obstructive market forces. And they were right; capital control is needed to protect that space. Free movement of capital creates what's sometimes called a "virtual parliament," a parliament of investors and lenders who have veto power over government decisions, sharply restricting democratic options. Actually, I'm quoting from technical papers in the economics literature. Free capital movement creates what's called a "dual constituency." Namely, voters as one constituency, and investors and lenders as the other constituency. And the investors and lenders conduct "moment by moment referendums" on government policy. If they don't like a policy because it's harming them, they veto it by withdrawing capital from that country or attacking the currency. And of course, the second constituency, the investors and lenders, prevails over the first constituency. The voters can't compete with them, even in the rich countries. And that's one of the most striking differences between the current phase of globalization and the phase before World War I.

Again, this is well understood. Let me just quote from a standard history of the international financial system by a highly-regarded American economist, Barry Eichengreen. He points out that before World War I, government policy had not yet been "politicized" by universal male suffrage and the rise of trade unions and parliamentary labor parties. Therefore, the very severe costs of market discipline, the costs imposed by the virtual parliament, could be transferred to the general population. Notice that the logic is exactly the same as that of structural adjustment in poor countries today: you impose the costs on the poor, and they can't do anything about it. Now, that's the way it was a hundred years ago. But that luxury was no longer available during the more democratic Bretton Woods period, after the Second World War. There was universal male suffrage, and parliamentary labor parties and unions, and furthermore the world population was very radical at that time. People had been greatly radicalized by the war, and there was enormous popular support, including in the United States, for a welfare state program. Therefore, it was necessary to do something. What Eichengreen points out is that limits on capital mobility substituted for limits on democracy as a source of insulation from market pressures, which is quite true. The limits on capital mobility allowed democracy to function. He doesn't follow the argument to the next step, but we easily can. Dismantling the Bretton Woods agreement should lead and has led to a sharp attack on substantive democracy, just as you would expect. This is particularly striking in the United States and Britain, which are in the lead on this, but in fact it's happening worldwide.

This attack on democracy is a very significant feature of the current phase of globalization. And there are other components of the "Washington consensus" with the same consequences. The basic idea of neoliberalism is to shift decisions, socioeconomic decisions, to unaccountable concentrations of power. That's a central feature of the neoliberal reforms, privatization for example. But remember, the powerful state remains to protect the masters. They need state protection. Another attack on democracy is being negotiated right now, in secret as always, at the Geneva negotiations on GATS (General Agreement on Trade and Services). What is this general agreement on trade and services? What are these "services"? Services are anything that could be within the public arena: education, health, welfare, water resources, communication, anything like that. There's no meaningful sense in which what is at stake is "trade in services." It's just called "trade" so that you can put it under the trade agreement. If you privatize these government services, you can have a perfectly functioning democracy, and it will do nothing, because nothing is left in the public arena. So privatizing services, which is what these negotiations are about, essentially eliminates from the public arena anything (or virtually anything) that might be subject to popular decision-making. That's called "trade in services," and naturally you have to negotiate that in secret. To the extent that anything leaks out about it, there is a huge public uproar.

The importance of protecting the public from information was revealed very dramatically at the April Summit of the Americas. Every editorial office in the United States had on its desk two major publications, which were timed for release at the summit. One was by Human Rights Watch, the main human rights organization in the US. The second was by the Economic Policy Institute, a major economic analysis institute in Washington. Both studies investigated in depth the effects of NAFTA on working people in the three countries (the United States, Canada and Mexico). Now, NAFTA was presented at the summit as a tremendous triumph, that's what George Bush said, and that's how the headlines read, and it's very easy to see why both studies were totally suppressed. The Human Rights Watch report described, in extensive detail, how labor rights were harmed in all three countries. The Economic Policy Institute report studied in detail how the wages, working conditions, etc., of working people were harmed in all three countries. This is one of those rare trade agreements which succeeded in harming everybody, in all three countries, at least apart from the people who count – they did fine.

If you look at the effects on Mexico, they are particularly instructive for countries like India, or for any place in the South. There, the effects of NAFTA were particularly severe. In fact, Mexico began the neoliberal reforms about twenty years ago, and wages have declined steadily since then. That continued after NAFTA, with a twenty-five percent decline for salaried workers and a forty percent decline for the self-employed. And these are underestimates, because they don't take into account the fact that the number of unsalaried workers increased greatly. So the actual effects were even worse. Foreign investment, for its part, grew after NAFTA – big headlines. There were no headlines for the fact that total investment declined. So foreign investment went up, but domestic investment went way down, and the economy was transferred into the hands of foreign multinationals. The minimum wage lost fifty percent of its purchasing power. Manufacturing declined and development stagnated, it may have reversed. Meanwhile, trade between the US and Mexico did increase. However, this increase related mainly to the component of trade that is internal to a firm, and that is centrally administered by a totalitarian system. That's called "trade" by economists, but it is not trade in any meaningful sense. If General Motors moves something to Mexico to be assembled and sends it back to the United States for sale, that's not trade. If you discount that, trade between Mexico and the United States may well have declined after NAFTA. Agriculture suffered a particularly severe blow for the usual reasons: Mexican farmers can't compete with highly subsidized US agribusiness. These findings confirm what had been reported in the business press and academic studies, and the story is familiar around the world.

Most of this had been predicted by critics of NAFTA, but they were wrong in one respect. Most critics, including me, anticipated that there would be a sharp increase in Mexico's urban-rural ratio after NAFTA, as hundreds of thousands of peasants were driven off the land. In fact, this did not happen. The urban-rural ratio remained the same. The reason, apparently, is that conditions deteriorated so badly in the cities that there was a huge flight of people to the United States, from both countryside and city. And those who survived the crossing (many did not) work for very low wages, without benefits, under awful conditions. The effect is to destroy lives and communities in Mexico, but that's not counted when you measure the effects of trade agreements. And it improves the US economy. One study of the Woodrow Wilson Foundation points out that consumption in the United States is subsidized by impoverishment of farm workers both in the United States and in Mexico. So it's a benefit for the economy, for the health of the economy.

These are the costs of NAFTA and of neoliberal corporate globalization generally. But those are costs that professional economics chooses not to measure. It's a choice. You could measure those costs, if you wanted to. They're called "externalities." We don't count them. But even by the highly ideological standard measures, which dismiss these, the costs have been very severe. And from what I've read, I understand that the same is true in India. But none of this was allowed to disturb the celebration of NAFTA and the Free Trade Agreement at the Summit of the Americas. In fact, unless people are connected to activist organizations, they cannot know any of this. They may know in their own lives or in the lives of people near them, but they can't know that this is the general situation. And one effect of this is to make people feel like failures. There's a fairy-tale economy out there, but my income is declining, and the people around me work harder, and so on. So there must be something wrong with us. In fact, "us" happens to be almost everybody. For about seventy-five percent of the US workforce, wages have stagnated or declined over the last twenty-five years, and the only way incomes are kept up is by increasing working hours. That's globalization in the richest country in the world. People around the middle of the American working class – who are called middle-class Americans – work about a month extra a year per family just to keep wages stagnant. That's by now, perhaps, the highest workload in the industrial world.

That picture generalizes around the world, with some variations. The main exceptions are countries which did not follow "the religion that markets know best." I'm quoting here from the latest Nobel Prize Laureate in economics, Joseph Stiglitz, in an article he wrote just before he was appointed Chief Economist of the World Bank, a position which he did not keep very long, because he kept making such annoying statements. He was kicked out. But what he said is correct. The countries that didn't follow the religion that markets know best did succeed in extensive growth during the neoliberal period. Almost everywhere else, it was as I have just described, worse for countries like Mexico than for the United States.

Furthermore, this is expected to continue. If you look at the provisions of the World Trade Organization, they deprive countries of exactly the mechanisms that were used for development. All of them are based on market interference. There isn't a single rich, developed country that didn't rely crucially on extensive market interference. That holds from England up to the East Asian NICs (Newly Industrialized Countries), and the United States dramatically. If the United States had followed the principle of comparative advantage that the poor must accept under contemporary neoliberalism, it would now be exporting fish. It would certainly not be exporting textiles. The only way it could develop textiles was through extremely heavy protectionist barriers that kept superior British textiles out. Actually, the reason Britain was producing textiles is because it did the same thing to India. It imposed heavy duties to keep Indian textiles out, and not just textiles, but also ships, steel, iron, manufacturing, all sorts of things, because they couldn't compete. Meanwhile, India was compelled to follow liberal rules. It became what economic historians call "an ocean of liberalism," and the results are obvious. Countries like the United States couldn't have developed a steel industry, for the same reason. British steel was superior, just as Indian iron had been superior to British iron a century earlier, and it was changed the same way. And this goes right up to the present.

Often a military cover is used for this. The dynamic source of the US economy is under the cover of the military system. It's a massive state sector of the economy. That includes just about everything, the whole "new economy," you know, electronics, computers, internet, telecommunications. You just go through the list; it's mostly developed under a military cover. And if you look at the WTO rules, you'll notice that they have a way of dealing with this. They allow for what's called a national security exemption.

So you're allowed to violate the rules on grounds of national security. Okay, for Haiti that doesn't help much. But for the United States it helps quite a lot, because it includes virtually the whole economy. The whole economy can be developed within a national security exemption, by placing it under the cutting edge of the military, and that's exactly what is done. You can hear Alan Greenspan speaking about the wonders of the entrepreneurial economy and rugged individualism and so on, and he even lists examples of these things. If you look at these examples, every single one of them was developed in the state sector, extensively, over a long period. And it's inconceivable that he doesn't know this, this is common knowledge, but it's not the kind of information that people have the right to.

All this is dramatically clear from economic history. Just ask yourself the simple question: which countries developed? Well, the countries that developed were Europe, North America, Japan, a couple of the countries in the Japanese colonial system, and that's about it. The rest of the world not only didn't develop, but it was pretty much destroyed. There's a characteristic in common to the countries that developed – they maintained their sovereignty; they were not colonized. And the correlation is extremely close; there are few correlations like that in history. Countries that maintained their own sovereignty and were able to violate the rules and integrate themselves into the economic system on their own terms, many of them did develop. Countries that lacked sovereignty and were subjected to external control, with only marginal exceptions, did not develop. Again, it takes a lot of discipline for economists and other intellectuals not to notice this fact. It's quite striking. Under the contemporary versions, Britain succeeded in developing a textile industry by destroying the superior Indian textile industry, by protectionist devices and state intervention. But textiles were based on cotton, and cotton was cheap, and why was cotton cheap? Well, cotton was cheap because of an institution called slavery. Slavery is a rather severe market interference. But when you study market economies, you don't count that. You don't count the fact that there was a massive market interference, based on state violence of the most extreme kind, that kept the basic commodity cheap. Cotton was like oil today, and in fact, oil is kept cheap the same way. A huge part of the Pentagon budget is directed towards maintaining the price of oil within a certain range. A few studies count that about thirty percent of the oil price is a subsidy, and there are plenty of other energy subsidies. Well, those things just aren't counted.

But even if you take the things that are counted, the facts are very clear. Under the current version of traditional mechanisms, about half the population of the world right now is literally in receivership. That means their economic policies are managed by bureaucrats in Washington. But even in the rich countries, democracy is under attack by virtue of the shift of decision-making from governments, which may be partially responsible to the population, to private tyrannies that don't have those defects. They are unaccountable, so they're fine. Shift decisions to them, everything's great. And that has very striking effects.

Take, say, Latin America. Latin America has undergone a wave of democratization in the past fifteen years. Military dictatorships were replaced by democracies. But academic specialists who follow this closely have been observing for years that as democracy is extended in Latin America, disillusionment with democracy is increasing. And that trend continues. A recently-released study revealed that about half the population of Latin America would now support democracy, and about half would be willing to accept military dictatorship. The military dictatorships in Latin America were extremely brutal affairs, but after the wave of democratization about half the population wouldn't mind if they came back. And the reasons are very clear. They're reported, in fact, even in the business press. Commenting on this, the London *Financial Times* said that the reason is an alarming trend, which links declining economic fortunes with a lack of faith in the institutions of democracy. And the reason is that this much-praised new wave of democracy happened to coincide with neoliberal economic programs, which undermine democracy. So you get more formal democracy and more disillusionment with democracy. And indeed Latin America, which has followed the rules most religiously, has been one of the regions that had the worst economic record. It's a correlation that holds world-wide.

That also holds for the United States. I'm sure you read a lot about the big clamor about the "stolen election" of November 2000, you know those Florida votes, the Supreme Court, and so on. If you read closely you'll notice that there was a huge issue for the press and elite commentators: they were very surprised about the fact that the public just didn't care. The public expressed no concern over the fact that the election was stolen. And the reasons are very clear from extensive public opinion studies. They reveal that on the eve of the election (well, before the Florida shenanigans), about seventy-five percent of the population regarded the whole process as a farce. It was a game played by rich corporations who do the funding, party leaders who are all crooks, and the public relations industry, which is just crafting candidates to say things that you can't believe even if you can understand them. So who cares what happens? If it's stolen, what's the difference? It doesn't make any difference anyway. As these same studies reveal, there is a measure of what they call "helplessness," an inability to affect anything that happens. That's been going up very fast. It hit its highest level last November, with about half the population saying that people like us have little or no influence on what government does. That's a very sharp rise right through the neoliberal period. Where there are issues that separate the public from the business world, they simply don't appear on the agenda. Take international economic issues. The public has very strong feelings on this, and business has very strong feelings, but they're opposite feelings. Accordingly, these issues cannot arise in the campaign. The Free Trade Area of the Americas, for example, could not be mentioned in the campaign. And that's true in general of these things called "free trade agreements." Actually, the business press more accurately calls them "free investment agreements." That's what we ought to call them. The free investment agreements are opposed by the public, supported by the business world and elites generally, therefore they cannot appear as issues in electoral campaigns.

The constitutional system in the United States was actually designed, very consciously, to have this effect. James Madison, who was the main framer at the Constitutional Convention, explained that the goal of government is "to protect the minority of the opulent against the majority." To achieve this, he said, political power must be placed in the hands of the "wealth of the nation," men who can be trusted to secure "the permanent interests of the country," which are the rights of the property owners, and to defend these interests against what he called "the levelling spirit" of the general population. And that continues to the present. It takes various forms, but that same principle is a leading principle of progressive political thought. Technical political scientist-types who write about these things say that it is wrong to describe the United States as a democracy, it should be described as a polyarchy. That is, a system where elites rule and the public ratifies. The public is supposed to show up every couple of years and say, you make the decisions, and then go home and buy shoes or something like that. That's the ideal system, and from that point of view the November 2000 election didn't reveal a flaw of American democracy, but revealed its triumph. And that triumph has been greatly enhanced by the neoliberal programs.

Throughout all this, a crucial element is restriction of information. That's why there is a huge public relations industry. They tell you what they are doing, it's not a secret. Back in the 1920s, one of the founders of the PR industry (a kind of Roosevelt-Kennedy liberal) wrote in a classic manual that the goal of the industry is to regiment the public mind every bit as much as an army regiments the bodies of its soldiers. Indeed, that's necessary, you can't have democracy otherwise. Unless the population is totally regimented, you can't allow democracy, because the population will do what they want, and that won't be securing the permanent interests of the country, namely the rights of the rich who have to be protected from the majority. This is quite conscious, there's nothing secret about it. It's the standard political science literature, supported by major figures like Joseph Schumpeter, Walter Lippmann and others.

The struggle to impose that regime takes many forms, and it never ends. It's going to continue as long as there are high concentrations of power controlling decision-making. And it's only reasonable to expect the masters to exploit every opportunity that they have, at the moment the fear and anguish in the face of the terrorist attacks. But there's absolutely no reason to accept those rules, and fortunately many people are rejecting them. There has been a very impressive increase of opposition, in recent years, taking totally new forms. It mostly developed in the South, with the North joining recently. The masters of the universe are very scared. They recognize what is happening. The meeting in Qatar, I'm sure you know, is an expression of the fear that the public may become involved. If they could figure out how to meet in a space shuttle, they'd meet there. Just keep the public away, because it's too dangerous. Every time the public breaks through, there is panic in the business press, literal panic. They know their control is extremely fragile; it can be destroyed at any time. It's mainly a matter of not accepting the injunction to be passive and acquiescent, and realizing that power actually is in the hands of populations, particularly in the more free and democratic societies, where it's impossible to use really massive force and violence to suppress the general population. These popular movements are unprecedented in scale. There's been nothing like them in history, in the range of constituency and in international solidarity. And I think the future, to a very large extent, lies in their hands – and it's very hard to overestimate what is at stake.

Question and Answer Session

Moderator: *There are many questions, about fifty, so they've been classified into four broad categories. The first set of questions, Professor Chomsky, refers to the so-called "clash of civilizations." I'll read one of them, and there are several like that: "Do you think that the present conflict between the Taliban and the US and its allies can take the shape of a clash of civilizations, as expected by Samuel Huntington?" Along with that there are related questions about the concept of religious fanaticism, and how fundamentalist tendencies around the world can be stopped.*

Chomsky: Let's start with the first question, whether the US-Taliban confrontation has something to do with Huntington's thesis of the clash of civilizations. Remember the context of Huntington's thesis, the context in which it was put forth. This was after the end of the Cold War. For fifty years, both the US and the Soviet Union had used the pretext of the Cold War as a justification for any atrocities that they wanted to carry out. So if the Russians wanted to send tanks to East Berlin, that was because of the Cold War. And if the US wanted to invade South Vietnam and wipe out Indochina, that was because of the Cold War. If you look at the history of this period, the pretext had nothing to do with the reasons. The reasons for the atrocities were domestically based in power interests, but the Cold War gave an excuse. Whatever the atrocity carried out, you could say it's defense against the other side.

After the collapse of the Soviet Union, the pretext is gone. The policies remain the same. In fact, the policies continue about as before, with slight changes in tactics, but you need a new pretext. In fact, there's been a search for pretexts for quite a long time. Actually, it started twenty years ago. When the Reagan Administration came in, it was already pretty clear that the pretext of the Russian threat was not going to work for very long. So they came into office saying that the focus of their foreign policy would be to combat the plague of international terrorism. That was twenty years ago. There's nothing new about this. We have to defend ourselves from other terrorists. And they proceeded to react to that plague by creating the most extraordinary international terrorist network in the world, which carried out massive terror in Central America and southern Africa and all over the place. In fact, it was so extreme that its actions were even condemned by the World Court and Security Council. With 1989 coming, you needed some new pretexts. And it was very explicit. Remember, one of the tasks of intellectuals, the solemn task, is to prevent people from understanding what is going on. And in order to fulfill that task, you have to ignore the government documentation, for example, which tells you exactly what's going on. And this is a case in point.

Just to give you one illustration. Every year, the White House presents to Congress a statement of why we need a huge military budget. Every year, it used to be the same: the Russians are coming. The Russians are coming, so we need this monstrous military budget. The question that anyone who is interested in international affairs should have been asking himself or herself is what are they going to say in March 1990? That was the first presentation to Congress after the Russians clearly weren't coming – they were not around anymore. So that was a very important and extremely interesting document. And of course, it is not mentioned anywhere, because it's much too interesting. That was March 1990, the first Bush administration giving its presentation to Congress. It's exactly the same, as every year. We need a huge military budget. We need massive intervention forces, mostly pointed at the Middle East. We have to protect what's called the "defense industrial base" – that's a euphemism for high-tech industry. We have to ensure that the public pays the costs of high-tech industry by funneling it through the military system, under the pretext of defense. So it's exactly the same as before. The only difference was the reasons. It turned out that the reason we needed all this was not because the Russians were coming, but – I'm quoting – because of the "technological sophistication of Third World powers." That's why we need the huge military budget. The massive military forces aimed at the Middle East still have to be aimed there, and here comes an interesting phrase. It says that they have to be aimed at the Middle East, where "the threat to our interests could not be laid at the Kremlin's door." In other words, sorry, I've been lying to you for fifty years, but now the Kremlin isn't around anymore, so I've got to tell you the truth: the threat to our interests could not be laid at the Kremlin's door. Remember, it couldn't be laid at Iraq's door either, because at that time Saddam Hussein was a great friend and ally of the United States. He had already carried out his worst atrocities, like gassing Kurds and everything else – but he remained a fine guy, hadn't disobeyed orders yet, the one crime that matters. So nothing could be laid at Iraq's door, or at the Kremlin's door. In fact, the threat had to be laid right at the door where it always had been: subjugated nations might take control of their own destiny, including their own resources. And that can't be tolerated, obviously. So we have to support brutal, oppressive states like Saudi Arabia and others, to make sure that they guarantee that the profits from oil – it's not so much the oil as the profits from oil – flow to the people who deserve it: rich western energy corporations or the US Treasury Department or Bechtel Corporation, and so on. So that's why we need massive military forces. Other than that, it's the same.

What does this have to do with Huntington? Well, he's a respected intellectual. He can't say this. He can't say, look, it's exactly the same as before. It's always the method by which the rich run the world, and the major confrontation remains what it has always been: small concentrated sectors of wealth and power versus everybody else. You can't say that. And, in fact, if you look at those passages on the clash of civilizations, he says that in the future the conflict will not be on economic grounds. So let's put that out of our minds. You can't think about rich powers and corporations exploiting people, that can't be the conflict. It's got to be something else. So it will be the "clash of civilizations" – the western civilization and Islam and Confucianism.

Well, you can test that. It's a strange idea, but you can test it. You can test it, for example, by asking how the United States, the leader of the western civilization, has reacted to Islamic fundamentalists. Well, the answer is, it's been their leading supporter. For instance, the most extreme Islamic fundamentalist state in the world at that time was Saudi Arabia. Maybe it has been succeeded by the Taliban, but that's an offshoot of Saudi Arabian Wahhabism. Saudi Arabia has been a client of the United States since its origins. And the reason is that it plays the right role. It ensures that the wealth of the region goes to the right people: not people in the slums of Cairo, but people in executive suites in New York. And as long as they do that, Saudi Arabian leaders can treat women as awfully as they want, they can be the most extreme fundamentalists in existence, they're just fine. That's the most extreme fundamentalist state in the world.

What is the biggest Muslim state in the world? Indonesia. And what's the relation between the United States and Indonesia? Well, actually the United States was hostile to Indonesia until 1965. That's because Indonesia was part of the Non-Aligned Movement. The United States hated Nehru, despised him in fact, for exactly the same reason. So they despised Indonesia. It was independent. Furthermore, it was a dangerous country, because it had one mass-based political party, the PKI, which was a party of the poor, a party of peasants, basically. And it was gaining power through the open democratic system; therefore it had to be stopped. The US tried to stop it in 1958, by supporting a rebellion. That failed. Then they started supporting the Indonesian army. And in 1965, the army carried out a coup, led by General Suharto. They massacred hundreds of thousands, maybe a million people (mostly landless peasants) and wiped out the only mass-based party. This led to unrestrained euphoria in the West. The United States, Britain, Australia – it was such a glorious event that they couldn't control themselves. The headlines were, "A gleam of light in Asia," "A hope where there once was none," "The Indonesian moderates have carried out a boiling bloodbath," "The greatest event in history." I mean, they didn't conceal what happened – staggering mass slaughter. The CIA compared it to the massacres of Stalin and Hitler, and that was wonderful. Ever since that time, Indonesia has been a favored ally of the United States. It continued to have one of the bloodiest records in the late twentieth century (mass murder in East Timor, hideous tortures of dissidents, and so on), but it was fine. It was the biggest Islamic state in the world, but it was just fine. Suharto was "our kind of guy," the way Clinton described him when he visited in the mid-1990s. And he stayed a friend of the United States, until he made a mistake. He made a mistake by dragging his feet over IMF orders. After the Asian crash, the IMF imposed very harsh orders, and Suharto didn't go along the way he was supposed to. And he also lost control of the society. That's also a mistake. So at that point, the Secretary of State, Madeleine Albright, gave him a telephone call and literally said, "We think it's time for a democratic transition." Four hours later, merely by accident, he abdicated. But Indonesia remained a US favorite state.

So that's two of the Islamic states. What about the most extreme Islamic fundamentalist non-state actors? Let's say the Al Qaeda network. Who created them? That's the creation of the CIA, British intelligence, Saudi Arabian funding, Egypt, and so on. They brought the most extreme radical fundamentalists they could find anywhere in north Africa and the Middle East – trained them, armed them, nurtured them to harass the Russians, and not to help the Afghans. These guys were carrying out terrorism from the very beginning (they assassinated President Sadat twenty years ago), with the support of the United States. So where is the clash of civilizations?

Let's move a little further. During the 1980s, the United States carried out a major war in Central America. A couple of hundred thousand people were killed, four countries almost destroyed, I mean it was a vast war. Who was the target of that war? Well, one of the main targets was the Catholic Church. The decade of the 1980s began with the assassination of an archbishop. It ended with the assassination of six leading Jesuit intellectuals, including the rector of the main university. They were killed by basically the same people – terrorist forces, organized and armed and trained by the United States. During that period, plenty of church people were killed. Hundreds of thousands of peasants and poor people also died, as usual, but one of the main targets was the Catholic Church. Why? Well, the Catholic Church had committed a grievous sin in Latin America. For hundreds of years, it had been the church of the rich. That was fine. But in the 1960s, the Latin American bishops adopted what they called a "preferential option for the poor." At that point, they became like this mass-based political party in Indonesia, which was a party of the poor and the peasants, and naturally it had to be wiped out. So the Catholic Church had to be smashed.

Coming back to the beginning, just where is the clash of civilizations? I mean, there is a clash alright. There is a clash with those who are adopting the preferential option for the poor, no matter who they are. They can be Catholics, they can be communists, they can be anything else. They can be white, black, green, anything. Western terror is totally ecumenical. It's not really racist – they'll kill anybody who takes the wrong stand on the major issues. But if you're an intellectual, you can't say that. Because it's too obviously true. And you can't let people understand what is obviously true. You have to create deep theories that can be understood only if you have a PhD from Harvard or something. So we have a clash of civilizations, and we're supposed to worship that. But it makes absolutely no sense.

Moderator: *Firstly, people seem to be very keen to know what you see as an alternative. What kinds of people's movements do we need, and is there any hope of breaking this concentration of power and influence? That's one. As for the other set of questions, I'll just read one, which captures many others: "How many students whom you have taught continue to follow or act upon your teachings? And in essence, is there some kind of mass hypnosis, or what kind of reaction do you get to your speeches in the United States?"*

Chomsky: Well, the second question is easier, so let me start with that. I teach graduate courses in linguistics and philosophy at the Massachusetts Institute of Technology. I've been involved in things like this most of my life. I've been involved in resistance, in and out of jail, all sorts of things. But I don't let it interfere with teaching. So it does not enter into my teaching. If students know about that side of my life, it's because they come to talks, or read what I write, or something. So essentially, the influence on students, say, in my own department is the same as it is everywhere else. It's nothing to do with anything that happens in a graduate seminar. You can argue about this approach, but in my view that's the way it ought to be done. Anyhow, that's what I've done.

As for my influence on others, well, you know the way the United States works. It's a very free country. There is very little state repression by comparative standards, especially if you're more or less privileged, as I am, like most of us are. But you can be excluded. So you're excluded from the mainstream, especially the parts that are more to the left-liberal side. Those are the real connoisseurs. They have to make sure that you go this far and not one millimeter further. So there are blocks. On the other hand, there are plenty of opportunities to reach other people. I mean, a few days before I came here, I gave a talk in Boston which had an audience of about two or three thousand people and was broadcast live over the internet, and all sorts of things. And that goes on all the time. And it's not just me. It's other people who spend their lives the same way. So there's very large outreach. Today's gathering is also part of it. This doesn't create popular movements by any means. In fact, it responds to them. It's the popular movements that create the opportunities for things like this. All these hundreds of talks I give all over the place are organized by somebody; they're organized by local people who are carrying out some kind of work. It may be with women or working people or the homeless or immigrants or a million other things, and they want somebody to come and give a talk for a fundraiser, or take part in a demonstration, whatever it may be. Those are the opportunities, and they reach huge numbers of people. It is because of these activities that the country has changed radically in the last thirty or forty years. It's a totally different country, much more civilized than it was forty years ago. That's why the sixties are so hated, so denounced in elite discussion. The reason is that they had a very substantial civilizing effect on the society, in many different ways. Women's rights, environmental issues, opposition to aggression, the anti-nuclear movement, and so on – all this goes back to the sixties. It was there before, but it really took off after the sixties.

In fact, a striking indication of this civilizing effect of the sixties is that this is the first time in US history, after hundreds of years, that some attention was paid to the fate of the indigenous population. Remember, that country was built on massive ethnic cleansing. Millions of people were exterminated. There were 7 or 8 million indigenous people, maybe more. They're not around anymore. They were just exterminated. And this was never an issue, never discussed. Textbooks, if they talked about it, praised it. When I grew up, as a kid we would play cowboys and Indians, where we were the cowboys, and we'd kill the Indians. That was just normal. The leading diplomatic history of the United States, by Thomas Bailey, a liberal historian writing in 1969, describes how the colonists, after kicking out the British, turned to their next task, namely "felling trees and Indians and expanding their natural borders." So there were trees in the way, and there were Indians in the way, and we sort of knocked them all down and expanded the national borders. That wasn't considered an odd thing to say at that time. I mean, it's so deeply rooted that some of the things that happened are mind-boggling. For example, think about the Israeli helicopters being used to assassinate Palestinian political leaders. Two questions: Where did the helicopters come from? Israel doesn't produce helicopters. They were sent by Clinton and Bush for that purpose, knowing that that's what they are for. Furthermore, what's the name of the helicopters? Tomahawk, Apache, that sort of thing. In fact, the weapons of war in the United States are named after the victims of genocide. If in Germany these days they named the helicopters of the Luftwaffe "Jew" and "Gypsy," people would think there's something wrong with that culture. But this goes on, and nobody notices it. Well, thirty years ago nobody would have noticed it. Now, some people do notice it. And there is some concern over what happened. That's part of the civilizing effect of the sixties.

And out of this grew mass popular organizations of all kinds. The Central American solidarity movements of the 1980s were something completely new in the history of imperialism. First of all, they were huge. Secondly, people didn't just protest. They didn't just have demonstrations. They went and lived with the victims. There were people who went and lived in Salvadoran villages, partly in the hope that they could help, but also because they thought that perhaps if there is a white face around it will restrain the state terrorists that their own country was organizing. This had never happened before. I mean, in no imperial war that I can remember did massive numbers of citizens go to protect the victims of their own country. That level of engagement is quite new. Thirdly, it's also interesting that this was not coming from the left. Some of it was, but not most of it. In fact, it was mainly rooted in conservative Christian mainstream communities, many of them were fundamentalists – in fact, Christian fundamentalists. It was very deeply rooted in mainstream US society, right out of main street Iowa. And it was very courageous and very honorable, something totally new. Well, that's another reflection of the same developments.

And this does not come from nowhere. We all know where it comes from. It comes from people organizing in their own community, or their own workplace, or whatever group they happen to be involved in, integrating with one another, making bigger organizations, linking up. By now, the linkages are worldwide. The major movements, by far, are in the South, in countries like India, and Brazil, and others. They're not noticed much in the West, because who cares what those people are doing, but that's the source of the anti-corporate globalization movement and plenty of other things. I don't have to tell you, you know way more about it than I do. That's the way things change. Every significant change in history has come about that way. And the next ones will too. And I think the next big changes are closer than we think, because the system of domination is extremely fragile, as I mentioned. And they know it. That's why it is based on such extensive secrecy. If you let people know what's going on, it's going to collapse. That can hold together for a while, but it's a fragile system, and we know just how to change it – by popular organization. It's not just a matter of opposing what's going on, but also of creating – I'll quote Bakunin – "the facts of the future in the present society." You build up the kinds of institutions that should exist in the future society, and let them begin to work and to flourish. Whether they are workers' control in industry, or cooperative villages, or women's groups, whatever they may be. Start building them. Let them work and function, and they'll be the future, once concentrated power is so weakened that it can't survive. How you get the changes, you can't predict, but that's the path that's worked in the past. That's why we don't live under feudalism, and slavery, and all kinds of horrors of the past that are mostly gone. And that's the way you go on.

Moderator: *The fourth set of questions focuses on globalization. Here is one that subsumes many others: "What do you think would be the effect if India continues with the present policies of globalization and integration with the global economy?"*

Chomsky: What would be the effect if India continues with accepting neoliberalism and integrating into the global economy on neoliberal terms? Well, I think there are a couple of centuries of history that give you an answer to that. There are differences of course, but in many ways that's what happened since the eighteenth century. England imposed a very liberal regime on India. Meanwhile, England itself maintained a very powerful state, the most powerful in Europe, with very high protection. Its labor management system was also quite different from India's; in fact, there is some very interesting scholarly work just coming out on this. The Cambridge University series on Indian history and society has just published a book by Prasannan Parthasarathi, based on a Harvard dissertation, I forget the title, but it's about weavers in South India in the eighteenth century. By the early nineteenth century, the weaving economy in South India was a total disaster story. The bones of the weavers were bleaching the plains of India, and all that. In the eighteenth century, they were doing quite well. In fact, his investigations show, fairly convincingly, that they were better off than workers in England. They had higher purchasing power. They had much more control of their work. They were mobile. This was ended by British state power. The British came in first through the East India Company, which basically was a state outfit, and then just by force, and they introduced British-style labor management rules. That meant cutting back mobility, so that workers can't resist by going somewhere else, imposing tight restrictions, breaking down the market relations which did exist in India. And that smashed the weavers. So within a century you get a disaster, which still continues. And if you look at history, that's the way it has been. Countries that were compelled to adopt real market principles were destroyed, and those that were able to control their own destiny by resisting colonization, and invariably relied quite heavily on state intervention for development (often in brutal ways), those countries developed.

If India decides to go back to what it was in the eighteenth century, you can predict what will happen. Right through the Raj, there was a sector of Indian society that was very wealthy. The Raj was run by Indians, not by the British. The British were in the background, but the place was mostly run by Indians, even the army. Until the 1857 Anglo-Indian war, the army was mostly sepoys. They were controlling the Indian population. Furthermore, that's the way it is in every other country too. So there'll be a sector of Indian society that will do fine. Most of the population will suffer. The general economy will be reliant on outsiders, won't be able to control itself. And you'll somehow probably relive the past. That's what I would suspect. On the other hand, of course, the world isn't the same as it was two hundred years ago, so it's not going to be a duplicate. But the patterns are pretty clear.

Just think about it, there's not a single society that is rich and developed today that followed liberal principles. Every single one of them radically violated them, including England. I mean, England did finally turn to free trade in 1846, but at that time England had already achieved twice the per capita capitalization of any other country, so the playing field looked level – you know, tilted in our direction. By that time, Indian manufacture had been pretty much destroyed. And even in the free trade period, England didn't rely on free trade. I mean, I think about forty percent of English exports went to India, its own colony. That's not free trade. When England could no longer compete with Germany in manufacturing, it still had the controlled Indian market. This continued until the 1920s. In the 1920s, England was no longer able to compete with Japanese manufacturing, so they simply called the whole game off. In 1932, England closed off the Empire, including India, to Japanese imports. That's part of the background for the Pacific War. The Dutch did the same in what was then the East Indies. The United States did the same in the Philippines. That's part of the background for the Second World War. I mean, everybody's perfectly happy with free trade, as long as we're going to win. If it looks like there's some problem, then you stop it.

The United States is the perfect example. I mentioned the national security exemptions. The national security exemptions in the WTO are just a way for the United States to have a very dynamic state sector, which is the innovative part of the economy, where the public pays the costs. Look at Ronald Reagan – nobody was more full of passionate rhetoric about free trade than the Reaganites. Yet they were the most protectionist government in postwar US history. They doubled the barriers to imports. They were bitterly denounced by the General Agreement on Tariffs and Trade (GATT), the predecessor of the WTO, for having led the assault against free trade. But that didn't stop them from spouting the wonders of free trade for other countries. And it's the same right up to the present.

Moderator: *We'll end with two questions from the press. The first one is: "Mr. Chomsky, could you tell us something about the depoliticization process associated with the involvement of Non-Governmental Organizations and funding agencies in Third World countries?"*

Chomsky: Yes, I understand. Well, I mean, all of you know, it's a very double-edged kind of business. There are many NGOs that do really good things. On the other hand, one effect of the NGOs, quite commonly, is to take decisions away from the communities, and also to give the state an excuse not to be concerned with the things it ought to be concerned with, like health and education and so on. Serious NGOs, those that are concerned with authentic development and democratization and rights (a lot of them are just kind of power agencies, agencies of some state, or corporations, or whatever), have to be very wary of this. They should follow the lead of the communities, not dictate to them. And they should not provide a means for the governing authorities to transfer power to corporations and say, we're not going to care about health and welfare. And there's no simple answer. I mean, they deal with these things in different ways. Some of them, I think, do pretty well. Like, take Oxfam. As far as I'm aware, around the world, it's handled these problems reasonably well. In other cases, the results are not so good.

Moderator: *Here is the final question, again from the press: "Do you suggest some change in the political system? You oppose democracy, you oppose communism, so what kind of political system should we have so that all these issues are taken care of?"*

Chomsky: Well, I think democracy might be a good idea. This reminds me of a statement attributed to Gandhi. I don't know if he actually said it or not, but he is supposed to have been asked what he thought of western civilization, and to have answered, "It would be a good idea." And I think you can say the same about democracy. True, functioning democracy, meaning local control of decision-making in every structure (community, a workplace, a collective, a peasant association, whatever), that should be the basis of a decent, reasonable society, with further integration and federation from the bottom up, as is feasible and beneficial, all the way to international organizations. This is just the traditional anarchist idea. It's not a novel idea; I'm not saying anything new. And it's the natural direction in which a commitment to democracy ought to lead, I think. There are plenty of barriers to it, but they can be overcome. In fact, just think of the barriers. In the twentieth century, three forms of totalitarianism developed: Bolshevism, fascism, and corporations. They really are three forms of totalitarianism. And in fact they have the same, pretty much the same intellectual roots. They come out of neo-Hegelian ideas about the rights of organic entities over individuals – a big attack on classical liberalism. Well, two of those forms of totalitarianism were overthrown. The third one is rampant. But it's no more engraved in stone than the other two. In fact, I think it's weaker. It doesn't have the same kind of coercive force behind it. So it can be overthrown, too, in favor of democratic control.

Appendix: An Interview with Noam Chomsky*

NOAM CHOMSKY, eminent linguist and social critic, visited India in January 1996 and gave a series of lectures in Delhi, Calcutta, Hyderabad, Madras and Thiruvananthapuram. His visit, sponsored by the Centre of Development Economics at the Delhi School of Economics in collaboration with *Frontline*, the Centre for Applied Linguistics and Translation Studies (University of Hyderabad), the Indian Institute of Technology (Madras) and the Centre for Development Studies (Thiruvananthapuram), has been rightly described as a major intellectual event. Speaking on a wide range of subjects, from democracy and human rights to the role of intellectuals in society, he captivated audience after audience with his lucid challenge of accepted political analyses, his uncompromising commitment to social equality and individual freedom, the breadth of his scholarship, and the engaging style of his lectures. Back at the Massachusetts Institute of Technology, he responded by email to some questions relating to the major themes of his India lectures.

The World Order

What do you mean exactly when you say that democracy and human rights are under attack in many countries?

I'll keep to the US, by far the most important case because of its enormous power and because it represents itself, and is regarded (not without reason) as in the forefront of the defense of democracy and human rights.

---
* First published in *Economic and Political Weekly*, vol. 13, no. 31 (30 March 1996), available at http://www.epw.in/commentary/chomsky-india-interview.html

http://dx.doi.org/10.11647/OBP.0050.06

Before turning to the factual questions, we have to clarify what we mean by "democracy" and "human rights." In the latter case, there is an international standard: the UN Universal Declaration of Human Rights (UD, December 1948), recognized by US courts as "customary international law," hence binding on the US government. On democracy, the issue is more complex. The UD is solemnly acclaimed by all states though supported by none, to my knowledge. The US, for example, has one of the worst records in the world even in ratifying international conventions designed to implement the UD, and its few ratifications are conditioned so as to make them unenforceable. Contrary to much pretense, the US denies the universality of the UD: specifically, it rejects all Articles pertaining to socio-economic rights. These facts, not controversial, passed virtually without comment during the impressive accolades for US leadership at the Vienna conference of 1993 celebrating the UD, where Washington thundered against the "Third World relativists" who dare to question its universality.

Turning to the parts of the UD that the US at least claims to support, we also find instructive gaps. Consider Article 14, which states that "Everyone has the right to seek and to enjoy in other countries asylum from persecution"; Haitians, for example, locked into a prison of terror and torture by an illegal US blockade while Washington was producing impressive rhetoric at the Vienna conference, indeed returned to that torture chamber by force during its proceedings.

Or consider Article 13, by far the best known provision of the UD, in the US. It states that "Everyone has the right to leave any country, including his own, *and to return to his country*" (my italics). This Article was invoked annually on Human Rights Day, December 10, with demonstrations led by distinguished law professors and civil libertarians issuing angry appeals to the Soviet Union to let Russian Jews leave. To be exact, *half* of Article 13 achieved such fame and renown; the words italicized were invariably omitted, for the simple reason that they are forcefully rejected by those who condemned the Soviet Union for its violations of the first half of Article 13. The significance of the omitted words was spelled out on December 11, 1948, the day after the UD was passed, in UN Resolution 194, also passed unanimously, which affirms the right of Palestinian refugees who had fled or had been expelled during the 1948 fighting to return to their homes. Resolution 194 continued to be endorsed by the US until 1993, when the Clinton administration broke from the traditional (and purely formal) advocacy of Resolution 194, voting alone (with Israel) against it; as usual, there was no report in the press.

This last example is a minor one in the general context of human rights violations, though it does illustrate with some clarity the utter hypocrisy of the advocacy of human rights: advocated with much passion as a weapon against someone else, rarely otherwise.

Let's turn to the core Articles that the US endorses: so-called "anti-torture" rights. As repeated studies have shown, US foreign aid is highly correlated with torture – not because the State Department likes torture, but because it likes a "favorable business climate," and that is often improved by murder of priests working for the poor, torture of union leaders, massacre of peasants, etc. Hence the secondary correlation between aid and torture. That continues. The leading human rights violator in the western hemisphere, as one can learn from (unreported) inquiries by Amnesty International, Human Rights Watch, the Church and others, is Colombia, with a horrendous record of atrocities. It also receives half of US military aid and training for the hemisphere, increasing under Clinton, under pretexts taken seriously by no knowledgeable observer. Again, one will find nothing of this in the press or mainstream journalism.

The attack on human rights is systematic, rooted in institutional needs, and continuing. Sometimes the attack by Washington is far more direct and violent, as during the 1980s, when the US-run terrorist wars in Central America (condemned, irrelevantly, by the World Court and the UN Security Council) left hundreds of thousands of tortured and mutilated corpses and four countries in ruins, with dubious prospects for survival – to no slight extent a war against the Roman Catholic Church, which had dared to interpret the Gospels as implying a "preferential option for the poor." Or in Africa in the same years, where terrorist forces from South Africa backed by the US and UK caused more than 1.5 million dead and 60 billion dollars in damage from 1980 to 1988, under the rubric of "constructive engagement." Sometimes the methods are more indirect, for example, programs of "aid" and "development" that are not unrelated to the fact that 800 million people in the world suffer malnutrition and that 13 million children die each year from easily treatable diseases; or that such shocking conditions can even be found in the richest country in the world, with unparalleled advantages, as a result of conscious social policy. All of this in radical violation of the UD, not to speak of elementary moral principles.

Let's turn to democracy. Here we have to distinguish between the US record abroad and at home. The most instructive examples abroad are of course in the regions with greatest US influence: Latin America. Here the US has regularly overthrown parliamentary regimes and instituted the rule of brutal torturers, carried out or supported murderous terrorism, and turned potentially rich and productive areas into some of the world's worst horror chambers. The record was characterized accurately by one of the leading specialists on US policy and democracy in Latin America, Thomas Carothers, who writes as both a scholar and an insider, having been in the Reagan State Department, working on its "democracy enhancement" programs, which have received much acclaim. Carothers regards these as "sincere," but a "failure"; a remarkably systematic failure, as he concedes. Where US influence was least, there was progress towards democracy, resisted by the Reaganites though they claimed credit for it when it could not be stopped. Where US influence was greatest, progress was least, and the US was willing to tolerate "only limited, top-down forms of democratic change that did not risk upsetting the traditional structures of power with which the US has long been allied," radically antidemocratic structures, as he observes.

That continues today. The US fulminates impressively (and accurately) about Cuba's lack of democracy. Meanwhile it lauds democracy in Colombia, where there is even an independent political party. Since it was formed ten years ago, about 2,500 of its leading activists have been murdered, mostly by the state authorities and their paramilitary associates, including presidential candidates, mayors, and others – a small fraction of the victims of state terror in this stellar democracy. Nothing comparable can be attributed to Cuba. Again, all this passes without comment.

Turning to the US itself, it has perhaps the most stable democratic institutions in the world, but it is important to bear in mind the principles on which US democracy was founded. The constitutional system was based on the principle that the prime responsibility of government is "to protect the minority of the opulent from the majority," as Madison, the leading framer, explained at the Constitutional Convention. Therefore, he elaborated, power must be in the hands of the wealthy, while the public is fragmented and scattered so that the threat of democracy is reduced and the country can be "governed by those who own it," as declared by John Jay, the president of the Convention and first Chief Justice of the Supreme Court. With all the changes that have taken place over two hundred years, that principle has been maintained, and indeed reiterated, particularly in the twentieth century, when leading Wilsonian liberals (Walter Lippmann, Howard Lasswell, etc.) explained that the "ignorant and meddlesome outsiders" (the general public) have no business interfering in the public arena – their "function" is solely to lend their weight now and then to one of the "responsible men" (elections). That message was forcefully reiterated twenty years ago by the Trilateral Commission, representing the more liberal internationalist currents among elites from western Europe, Japan and the US, in their study *Crisis of Democracy*. The "crisis" was that during the ferment of the 1960s, the public began to depart from its normal apathy and passivity. The study recommends means to drive people back to their spectator role, so that "democracy" can be protected. Recall that this is the liberal side of the spectrum; the mislabeled conservatives are far more strongly opposed to democracy. Social policy and propaganda since have been directed to the goal of overcoming "the crisis of democracy" by sharply reducing participation in democratic institutions. The public grasps that in some manner; by now, an unprecedented eighty percent of the public regards American democracy as non-functional.

The major attack on democracy is the effort to shift decision-making even more than before into the hands of unaccountable private tyrannies: the corporate world, which is fundamentally totalitarian in character, as long understood by business historians and political economists. That is the goal of the current efforts to weaken those elements of the national government that serve public needs, while expanding those that serve business power, notably the Pentagon system, which was designed in large measure as a device to transfer public funds to advanced sectors of industry under the guise of "security," and continues to serve that function.

Another powerful weapon against democracy is the astronomical growth of financial capital, which is now able to undermine democratic national planning by transferring masses of capital away from countries that seek to depart from the preferred model of low growth, low wage, high profit social policy. Even the US is not immune: Clinton proposed a very mild economic stimulus in 1993, but withdrew it quickly under the threat of the bond market – though whether this was a necessity or a choice is another question.

There is much to say about these matters. Without placing them at the focus of attention, one is not discussing the real world. And that world is one in which human rights and democracy are under serious attack, not only from the recognized leader of "the campaign for democracy and human rights," but elsewhere as well.

Would you say that the attack on democracy and human rights applies in India, too? And if so why?

I would not presume to discuss India on the basis of my limited knowledge. But to answer your question: yes, I think so, for very much the same reasons, though, of course, the socioeconomic projects that undermine human rights and democracy have a much harsher impact in a country like India than in the US.

Is there a "new world order" after the Cold War? And if so, how does it differ from the old world order?

"New world orders" are constantly proclaimed, sometimes with reason. There was a substantial change, of course, with the Second World War. The most significant changes, in my opinion, were in the early 1970s. Nixon's dismantling of the Bretton Woods system was a major factor in the huge explosion of financial capital, enhanced by the telecommunications revolution and the sudden flow of petrodollars. The same tendencies contributed to a new phase of transnational capital, with actual or threatened transfer of production abroad. These developments have placed powerful new weapons in the hands of the private tyrannies that have been seeking to dismantle residual democratic forms and even to undermine markets, as we find if we take an honest look. The end of the Cold War, returning most of eastern Europe to its traditional role as a Third World service area, has provided still more weapons to private power. Huge conglomerates can now undermine what the business press calls the "luxurious life-style" of the "pampered western workers" not only by transferring operations to Mexico and Indonesia, but also to Poland and Hungary – of course demanding high tariff protection and other subsidy, on the usual interpretation of "free markets."

So yes, there is another phase of world order, with the same basic structure (because dominant institutions remain highly stable and unchallenged), though with modifications that are quite significant for human life: for example, for the majority of Americans, whose family incomes and security have been steadily declining for fifteen years, and for those elsewhere who suffer far more severely from the same developments.

How does the domestic political situation in the US today affect the rest of the world?

Since the Second World War, the US has been by far the richest and most powerful country in the world. While the recovery of Europe and Japan (with its periphery) created a more complex "tripolar" global economy, US power remained pre-eminent. The options for some measure of independence have declined markedly in the Third World, in part for the reasons just mentioned. Though it is hard to give a precise measure, it seems clear that US cultural and doctrinal influence is even more overwhelming than its economic power in much of the world, certainly western Europe, and much of the Third World too. In the light of such facts, anything that happens in the US is of great significance for the rest of the world.

What is your reading of the current "peace process" in West Asia?

The term "peace process" itself is an interesting reflection of US doctrinal hegemony. The facts are clear and uncontroversial. The June 1967 war brought the world close to dangerous superpower confrontation, and led to diplomatic efforts to resolve the Arab-Israel conflict. The result was UN 242 (November 1967), which established the principle of full peace in return for full Israeli withdrawal from conquered territories (with at most minor and mutual border adjustments). In the light of subsequent propaganda, it is important to stress that the US explicitly advocated this interpretation, which it helped craft, as demonstrated very clearly by the documentary record. The Arab states rejected full peace; Israel rejected full withdrawal.

The impasse was broken in February 1971 when President Sadat of Egypt accepted official US policy (and UN 242) with regard to Israel and Egypt, saying nothing about the West Bank and Golan Heights (or Palestinian rights, which at that time were unmentioned). Israel recognized this as a "genuine peace offer" but refused to withdraw. The US had to decide whether to persist with its official policy, or to support Israel. In the internal debate, Kissinger prevailed, and the US instituted his policy of "Stalemate" (his word): no negotiations, only force. That led directly to the 1973 war, which undermined the Israeli- Kissinger assumption that Egypt had no military option. US tactics were adjusted, aiming to neutralize Egypt so that Israel could continue to integrate the territories and attack Lebanon without fear of Egyptian reprisal. That is precisely what happened, with massive US support, as a result of the Camp David agreements (1978-79).

Meanwhile, by the mid-seventies the international consensus had shifted, now recognizing Palestinian rights in the West Bank and Gaza. From January 1976, the US has therefore, been compelled to veto Security Council resolutions, vote alone (with Israel, and occasionally some other client state) against annual General Assembly Resolutions, and block every other diplomatic initiative: from Europe, the Arab States, the PLO, the Third World, whatever.

In brief, from 1971, and even more clearly from the mid-1970s, the US has led the rejectionist camp, and has effectively blocked diplomatic efforts to resolve the conflict. In the US the crucial facts are entirely suppressed in the media and journals of opinion, often even in scholarship. These are instructive features of "free institutions" that are either owned outright by private tyrannies closely linked to state power or heavily dominated by them: admittedly a somewhat extreme case of voluntary subordination to power, though not unique. Washington's disruption of any diplomatic settlement is what is called "the peace process," a technical term that refers to whatever the US government happens to be doing, often blocking peace. The Gulf War established that "what we say goes" – George Bush's proud words as he proclaimed his "new world order." At last, the US was able to extend the Monroe Doctrine to West Asia, temporarily at least. Immediately after the Gulf War, the US initiated its own unilateral and rejectionist "peace process" at Madrid. This has been consummated in the Oslo Agreements, which effectively rescind UN 242 and all other relevant international agreements. Oslo II (September 1995) leaves Israel in full control of seventy percent of the West Bank and thirty percent of the Gaza Strip, and effective control of the rest, including the water and other resources. It retains "veto power" over the Palestinian Administration that is granted limited local autonomy and, in return for this gift, must recognize the legality of Israeli settlements in the territories and Israeli sovereignty over the parts it will choose to retain, unilaterally (thanks to US support). With huge US subsidies, Israel is expanding development projects designed to establish irrevocably a version of the programs it announced in 1968: to take over some forty percent of the territories and to leave the rest under effective Israeli control, but local (or Jordanian) administration. That is pretty much the traditional colonial pattern: the British in India, whites in southern Africa, etc.

The outcome is a dramatic reaffirmation of the rule of force in international affairs, and also of the power of American doctrinal institutions. I've been astonished to see the extent to which Europeans and Third World elites have accepted and internalized US propaganda, even forgetting positions they themselves had advocated only a few years ago. I was rather surprised to find that in India, though my experience is limited. There are important lessons here, which should be carefully considered.

Structural Adjustment

How do you interpret the current wave of structural adjustment programs in different countries?

The current wave of "neoliberalism," applied now to the rich societies as well, is in my opinion a reflection of the shift of power towards private tyrannies in the past twenty-five years. But we should bear in mind that there is nothing fundamentally new about "structural adjustment." For hundreds of years, what we might call "really existing free market doctrine" has had a dual form: for you, but not for me, except for temporary advantage. From England to the US to the "late developing" industrial societies and on to today's NICs, a crucial factor in development has been protection from market discipline. Import barriers are only one element of such protection; the US Pentagon system, to take only one case, has been a far more significant element in the past half-century. At the same time, market discipline has been imposed on those who could not resist it. Today's First and Third Worlds were much more similar in the eighteenth century; "really existing free market doctrine" is one factor in their sharp divergence since.

Today's "structural adjustment" is a new variant of the traditional dual conception of free markets. The Reagan administration produced most impressive odes to the wonders of the free market – for others. Meanwhile, it introduced more import barriers than all postwar administrations combined while pouring public funds into hi-tech industry under the usual pretext of "security," a conscious fraud as we know from the documentary record. Today's "conservatives" demand that hungry seven-year old children be denied free lunches at school so that they will learn "responsibility" and "family values." But their leader Newt Gingrich funnels to his super-rich constituents more federal subsidies than to any suburban district in the country apart from the Federal system itself; and the ultra-right Heritage Foundation, while calling for sharp cuts in government programs that serve the great majority, also demands an increase in the Pentagon budget, not because the US faces any threat, but because the "conservatives" understand well that advanced sectors of industry rely heavily on the nanny state. In material that reaches the public, including its educated sectors, one will have to search diligently for any hint of these elementary features of contemporary US society.

The latest phase of "free market doctrine" reflects the changes in power already mentioned. The principles themselves are familiar. As for the impact of these programs, it is mixed and complex, though some features are evident. Advocates of the "Washington consensus" concede that among the most important factors in development are relative equality and improvement of "human capital" (health, education, etc.), all radically undermined by the programs they demand. The World Bank also calls for a shift to agro-export and opening of markets to subsidize western agricultural imports, surely knowing that the effect is to place primary producers in competition with one another, with obvious consequences, and to undermine food production for domestic needs. The Bank's economists can also read the recent report of the FAO warning the poorer countries of the danger of failure to develop indigenous sources of food. Structural adjustment yields repeated "economic miracles" – as in Brazil, Mexico, and elsewhere. But it pays to look at their character.

Generalizations are of doubtful validity. Honest economists recognize that little is understood about these matters, and that a great deal depends on specific contingencies. There is, however, historical and contemporary evidence that should not be simply dismissed in favor of a theoretical apparatus based on unrealistic assumptions and with little empirical support; and – not coincidentally I think – that undergirds policies that are highly supportive of established power and privilege. One of the most consistent consequences of "structural adjustment," as of other "experiments" in social engineering back to the eighteenth century, is that the designers do very well, however others may suffer.

Do you have any views on India's own structural adjustment program?

As is well known, India has been undergoing forms of "structural adjustment" for most of its modern history – one reason why India is India, while England is England, having become willing to toy for a time with *laissez-faire*, after 150 years of protectionism and destruction of competitors had given it huge advantages. While development was barred by "free market principles" in India (and by British force in Egypt and elsewhere), the US was able to develop textiles, steel, and later a full modern economy by leading the world in protectionism and extensive state intervention in the economy. It is hard to miss the fact that the two parts of the South to develop are the two that escaped colonial rule and the market discipline it imposed: the US and Japan, with some if its colonies in tow. As for current policies, one has to evaluate them on their merits, in the light of the options available. That's a complex question, and one should be skeptical about the advice of self-proclaimed experts. I would not hazard any specific advice without closer study, and if I were to, no sensible person should pay any attention to it. The same holds far more broadly, in my opinion.

India in the World

In your assessment, where does India fit in the US foreign policy agenda?

In the postwar period, India was not a central issue in US policy. The US was strongly opposed to Nehru's neutralism and efforts at independent development. As recognized by diplomatic historians, the US brought the Cold War to South Asia by arming Pakistan, in large part out of concerns about West Asia, it seems. By the 1950s, and particularly in the Kennedy period, the US was becoming more concerned with the demonstration effect of Chinese development, and supported India as the "democratic alternative," though always with considerable reluctance because of India's relative independence and its links to the USSR. Today, the US hopes to incorporate India within the global system dominated by the TNCs (transnational corporations) and the powerful states in which they are based, and the quasi-governmental institutions taking shape around them: the international financial institutions, the World Trade Organization, G7, etc.

Do you support India having a permanent seat on the Security Council?

It's not a bad idea, but I think the matter is peripheral to the problems faced by the UN. The more fundamental question is whether the US (or any great power) will permit an independent voice in world affairs, one that it does not control. So far, the record on that is bleak, a reflection of the weakness of functioning democracy, in my opinion.

There is intense debate here, at the moment, about whether India should sign the Comprehensive Test Ban Treaty (CTBT). Do you have any comments on this?

That the CTBT is hypocritical at its core is plain enough. It is an attempt to keep a monopoly of force in the hands of the US and its allies – to the extent possible (thus Israel, a US client, is under no pressure to abandon its nuclear program, which the US has in fact supported). On the other hand, nuclear weapons are an extraordinary danger, and proliferation may spell the end of human life. Within such unpleasant but real conditions, India has to make choices. I don't feel in any position to give advice.

Socialism and Democracy

The end of the Cold War has been widely interpreted as the victory of capitalism over socialism. Is this accurate?

It is not only inaccurate, but ludicrous. First, there are no "capitalist" countries; rather various forms of state capitalism. Capitalism would hardly be able to survive, for reasons discussed by Karl Polanyi years ago; and the business world has never been willing to accept market discipline except for temporary advantage, always demanding state protection when needed. Merely to give one indication, a recent study of the hundred leading TNCs (reported in the London *Financial Times*) found that all had benefited from the intervention of the state in which they are based, and twenty "would not have survived" without such state support.

As for "socialism," Soviet leaders did call the system they ran "socialist" just as they called it "democratic" ("peoples democracies"). The West (properly) ridiculed the claim to democracy, but was delighted with the equally ridiculous pretense of "socialism," which it could use as a weapon to batter authentic socialism. Lenin and Trotsky at once dismantled every socialist tendency that had developed in the turmoil before the Bolshevik takeover, including factory councils, Soviets, etc., and moved quickly to convert the country into a "labor army" ruled by the maximal leader. This was principled at least on Lenin's part (Trotsky, in contrast, had warned years earlier that this would be the consequence of Lenin's authoritarian deviation from the socialist mainstream). In doctrinal matters, Lenin was an orthodox Marxist, who probably assumed that socialism was impossible in a backward peasant society and felt he was carrying out a "holding action" until the "iron laws of history" led to the predicted revolution in Germany. When that attempt was drowned in blood, he shifted at once to state capitalism (the New Economic Policy, or NEP). The totalitarian system he had designed was later turned into an utter monstrosity by Stalin.

At no point from October 1917 was there a willingness to tolerate socialism. True, terms of discourse about society and politics are hardly models of clarity. But if "socialism" meant anything, it meant control by producers over production – at the very least. There wasn't a vestige of that in the Bolshevik system.

The Cold War, in my opinion, falls to a large extent within the traditional "North-South conflict," to use the contemporary euphemism. Eastern Europe was the West's original "Third World," separating the West from pre-Columbian times; the West beginning to develop, the East becoming its service area. Russia was declining relative to the West until the First World War; much the same was true elsewhere in the region. Of course, Russia was a very unusual part of the Third World; thus the Czar had a huge and menacing military force. But the basic logic of the North-South conflict holds rather well. The service areas are to pursue only "complementary development," their primary "function" being to provide markets, investment opportunities, resources, cheap labor, and other amenities. The crime of independence becomes even more severe if it seems to be succeeding in terms that might influence others facing similar problems, in which case the criminal is termed a "rotten apple that might spoil the barrel," a "virus" that might "infect" others, etc. The Cold War began in 1918 (as reputable scholarship recognizes: George Kennan, for example). And for basically these reasons (as it does not recognize).

The logic is not fundamentally different from Grenada or Nicaragua, though the scale was radically different, so the conflict took on a life of its own. With the end of the Cold War, the *status quo ante* is being pretty much restored. Sectors of eastern Europe that were part of the industrial West (the Czech Republic, western Poland, etc.) are returned to it. Most of the rest is assuming standard Third World characteristics. These are only first approximations, of course, but fairly close ones, I think.

After the collapse of the communist regime in the former Soviet Union and eastern Europe, what are the prospects for socialism today?

The collapse of Soviet tyranny is a small victory for socialism, for the same reason that the collapse of fascism was. It removed a barrier to socialism. Or so it should be regarded, in my opinion. It isn't, because much of educated opinion worldwide succumbed to the illusions fostered by the world's two leading propaganda systems, which agreed in calling this radical attack on socialism "socialism" (the USSR, so as to gain what advantage it could from the moral appeal of socialism, the West, so as to defame socialism). That is tragic, but it should be within our power to reverse these gross misinterpretations.

What went wrong with the socialist program in "communist" countries?

There were never any socialist programs, so nothing could go wrong with them. As to what happened, we have to first settle the standards of evaluation. The usual standard is to compare eastern Europe with the West – which is about as sensible as comparing kindergartens in Boston with local universities, than grandly proving that the former is a failure because children there know less quantum physics than graduate students at the Massachusetts Institute of Technology. It is a remarkable comment of western intellectual life that this farce can even proceed.

If one wants to make sensible comparisons, one begins with countries that were at a more or less comparable state of development and prospects before the Bolshevik system was instituted: perhaps Russia and Brazil, or Bulgaria and Guatemala. Such comparisons, the only realistic ones, are notable by their absence; I've presented some in several books, but the only reaction has been silence or outrage. One can understand why. The Bolshevik system was a monstrosity, but a close look shows that what the US has done to the regions under its control is even worse, for the majority of the population, though the conditions for successful development were far more favorable.

That's not an acceptable conclusion, so what is offered is a comparison that scarcely rises to absurdity. Recall that Brazil, a country with enormous potential and vast advantages, was taken over by the US fifty years ago as a "testing area" for scientific methods of development, and was considered a great "success story" for American capitalism as recently as 1989. And Guatemala was going to be a "showcase for democracy and capitalism" after a US-run coup overthrew its first democratic government forty years ago and installed a regime of neo-Nazi killers who have been devastating the place since. And so on down the list. A look at the facts is instructive, too much so to be allowed to enter the canon.

The Bolshevik system of forced industrialization was a human catastrophe, and the totalitarian socio-political system prevented progress beyond early stages. By the 1960s, the economy was beginning to stagnate, harmed even more by the militarization program undertaken in response to the vast Kennedy program of armament and confrontation. As to what might have happened had the western reaction been different, one can only speculate.

Why does Leninism have so much appeal among revolutionary movements?

Leninism definitely has an appeal among those who declare themselves the leaders of revolutionary movements. As for its appeal among the actual movements, that's a different matter, not easy to determine without close inquiry that goes beyond the pronouncements of intellectuals. I'm skeptical. Anyway, the distinction is crucial.

Leninism declares that "radical intellectuals" should take control of popular movements and use their struggles to gain power, then rule with an iron hand. The consequences are hardly a surprise. They were predicted by Bakunin long before Lenin appeared on the scene, and Leninist doctrine was condemned for these reasons early in the century by Trotsky, Rosa Luxemburg, and intellectual leaders of the Marxist left like Anton Pannekoek and others. The effects were very quickly recognized by Luxemburg and Pannekoek, and by independent leftists like Bertrand Russell, and of course, by the libertarian left.

Why should this doctrine appeal to intellectuals who appear on the scene with the message of "I'm your leader"? The answer is pretty clear I'm afraid, and not very attractive.

Does libertarian socialism have any relevance for popular movements in the Third World today?

Libertarian socialism begins by recognizing, with all serious forms of socialism, that socialism will be free or it will not be at all. Beyond that, it consistently questions power and authority. It seems to me of great relevance to any person or popular movement interested in defending human rights and expanding the sphere of freedom and justice. That includes the First World as well.

Westerners have had it drilled into their heads that rule by private tyrannies is "freedom." In the US the power of this propaganda has been extraordinary. One illustration is the fate of the media. When radio appeared in the 1920s, in most countries it was placed under public authority, and was as democratic as the society was: zero in the USSR, quite considerable in the case of BBC. In the US, perhaps uniquely, it was handed over to powerful corporations, though not without a struggle. The takeover by private tyranny was supported by liberals and civil libertarians on the grounds that it contributes to democracy. After all, what could be more democratic than control by huge unaccountable corporations? The public relations industry, the world's major propaganda organization by far, is dedicated to that message. While in India, I happened to turn on the BBC World Service, and to my astonishment, saw a statement by the Advertising Council (part of the corporate propaganda system) explaining how commercial advertising creates freedom. What could we desire beyond freedom to choose between two commodities we don't want and can't afford?

Free minds should not succumb to this crude and vulgar propaganda. Unaccountable private tyrannies have no intrinsic rights, and expansion of their power is hardly a contribution to freedom. The rights they are granted are, it is true, extraordinary, but also rather recent, and without justification in my opinion – a conclusion that used to be close to a truism among popular movements and leading intellectuals.

Libertarian socialism, or anarchism, questions all kinds of power: state, private, personal, whatever. It is, in my view, a natural outgrowth of Enlightenment and classical liberal ideas that were wrecked on the rocks of emerging industrial capitalism, as Rudolf Rocker observed sixty years ago. I think these ideas have substantial validity. They naturally have to be reshaped to apply to today's world. But I think it makes good sense to adopt the principle that any form of authority carries a heavy burden of justification. If it cannot provide a justification, it is illegitimate, and should be dismantled. That's true of everything from personal relations to social, economic, and political institutions. Libertarian socialism is guided by this principle, and seeks to apply it to every domain of existence. That's not only of relevance, but of crucial significance for decent people everywhere, in my opinion.

In western countries, Marxism has lost much of its appeal, even in radical circles. In India, however, it continues to dominate revolutionary thought and action. How do you interpret this contrast?

Marxism is a curious notion like Freudianism. These are, in my opinion, forms of organized religion, which treat individuals as gods, or maybe idols. In disciplines that have passed beyond the most primitive stage, there is (or should be) nothing comparable. There is no "Einsteinism" in physics, for good reasons.

Marx was a human being, with virtues and faults. He had a good deal to say about many topics; incidentally, not socialism, about which he had only a few rather conventional remarks, as far as I know. Sane people will learn from him what they can, discarding what is wrong or irrelevant. The fact that Marxism, as a form of idolatry, has lost its appeal is all to the good. It is not to the good that it has been replaced by other forms of religious fundamentalism – a term that I am afraid applies all too well to much of what passes for "free market doctrine" and "neo-liberalism." In countries that are more effectively under the control of state capitalist doctrinal systems, "Marxism" was never very influential and has now pretty much disappeared. In countries that are less disciplined, it remains more influential. In my opinion, "Marxism" (though not Marx's work) should disappear everywhere, but not to be replaced by new dogma and secular religion; rather, by independent thought.

What are the positive insights we can gain from Marxism?

Marx had important things to say about economic history and contemporary affairs, and interesting ideas about a certain rather abstract model of capitalism. Certainly, what he wrote should be taken quite seriously, and one will learn from it what one can. Beyond that loose comment, it is a matter of looking closely at particular ideas and analyses, something I cannot attempt here. I should say that some of what I personally find most appealing in Marx, namely, the early manuscripts, is drawn rather directly from aspects of the Enlightenment and Romantic traditions that I think have much to offer, something I've written about.

How do you interpret the popularity of communist parties today in the former Soviet Union and eastern Europe?

We should distinguish two kinds of "communists" in eastern Europe. Some are the "Nomenklatura capitalists," rich beyond their wildest dreams as they assume the role of Third World elites. Others, no less opportunistic, are seeking power on the basis of the terrible human consequences of the huge social engineering projects that were designed by people who knew little about the society and were surely not relying on any well-established theoretical understanding – projects that, as usual throughout history, offer great advantages to the institutions that grant authority to the designers, and are called "reforms" because of the favorable connotation (we don't call Stalin's innovations "reforms"). The "reforms" may help the population or harm them, but that is incidental.

I doubt very much that eastern Europeans want to return to the Stalinist dungeon. Nevertheless, they increasingly regard the Brezhnev era as a kind of "golden age." Western-run polls are pretty clear about that, I don't think this is nostalgia for a disappearing past as much as it is recognition of what is approaching: Brazil and Mexico, and other long-term beneficiaries of tutelage by the industrial powers of the West. The historical pattern is not exceptionless. One striking exception is Japan, a brutal imperial power, which, however, developed its colonies rather than ruining them. Formosa (Taiwan) and Korea developed approximately as Japan itself did during the period of Japanese rule, a course of development that picked up again, under rather special circumstances, from the 1960s. The devil is very much in the details in such cases.

You are sometimes described as an anarchist, or as a libertarian socialist. Do you accept any of these designations? If not, how would you summarize your basic political beliefs?

I'm happy with the designation "libertarian socialist" or "anarchist," though like all terms of political discourse, these (particularly the latter) are used broadly and inconsistently. I frankly don't care much what term is used, and rarely use standard terminology at all because it has become so vulgarized. What's important is the ideas, analyses, and proposals, whatever one chooses to call them. And here there is plenty of complexity. Take myself. As an anarchist, I think that the state is fundamentally illegitimate and should be dismantled. But at the moment, I'm in favor of strengthening the federal government in the US – not the sectors, like the Pentagon, that are part of the welfare system for the rich, but other sectors that can be responsive to popular will and can stand as a barrier to private tyranny. That's not strictly a contradiction: rather, a reflection of the complexity of the real world.

Are there important practical experiences of libertarian socialism in recent history, and what can we learn from them?

There are very instructive applications. The most significant, I think, are the achievements of the anarchist revolution in Spain in 1936 before it was crushed by the combined forces of the communists, fascists, and western democracies. Like most civil strife, the Spanish civil war was not just a conflict between the official "two sides": in this case, the republic and the fascists. There was a "third side" that had deep popular roots after decades of organizing, education, and struggle. In this case, the "third side" was highly significant, with real achievements to its credit in industrial Catalonia, rural Aragon, and elsewhere. Though the popular revolution was demolished by force, its impact survived even through the brutal fascist repression that followed. I think one can detect this influence in the highly successful Mondragon worker-owned complex in the Basque country, the largest in the world, combining industry, banking and social and community services. Its immediate origins are in the left populist church, but it appears to have deeper anarchist roots.

One finds libertarian tendencies far more broadly. In the seventeenth century English revolutions, for example. Hannah Arendt once pointed out the spontaneous appearance of variants of council communism, anarchist in spirit, in almost all modern revolutions. One example she discussed was the Hungarian revolution of 1956, where the councils were crushed by Soviet tanks, much as in Spain twenty years earlier. Though I hesitate to draw conclusions from limited experience, my impression in the West Bengal panchayat I visited was that very similar tendencies have been taking shape, in part spontaneously, it seems. Green shoots of this nature arise all over the place, sometimes with considerable impact, which often withstand harsh repression. One can make a case that a good part of the progress of civilization reflects such popular tendencies.

Who are the great libertarian socialist thinkers, in your opinion, and what are their essential insights?

As you know, I'm not overly impressed by "great figures." Modern libertarian socialist thought has roots in the Enlightenment and classical liberalism, perhaps most strikingly Wilhelm von Humboldt. There were important contributions by Proudhon, Bakunin, Kropotkin, and many others, also by left Marxists like Luxemburg and Pannekoek, and leading twentieth-century philosophers like Bertrand Russell. But the most important contributions were in the constructive work done by people who have disappeared from history, who developed such ideas and applied them in labor organizing, educational and social activities of all kinds, and institutions they created and defended. The leading insights? The primary one, as old as the hills, is the illegitimacy of authority, unless it can be justified. That insight then works itself out in a critical analysis of all human relations and institutions, with consequences depending on time, place, and topic. Some have constructed very detailed pictures of how a libertarian society or "participatory economy" might work. The ideas are interesting, but I'm personally a bit skeptical about far-reaching programs. I don't think enough is understood about complex systems; even in the hard sciences, understanding drops off pretty quickly when we move much beyond big molecules. I think there is ample room for experimentation, and though I naturally have my own ideas as to where it might lead, I think the general principles are clearer than the specific applications, which simply have to be explored.

You have persistently highlighted how democratic institutions, in the US and elsewhere, tend to be systematically subverted by corporate interests and privileged classes. Does this mean that there is no point in engaging in democratic politics?

Elite opinion and the doctrinal institutions try very hard to discourage political participation, except for the very narrow matter of choosing among candidates representing one or another coalition of investors. They do so because of the fear of the potential of democratic politics, a leading theme of democratic principles and theory from the Founding Fathers of American democracy to the present, underscored again by the study of the Trilateral Commission that I mentioned. For the same reason, people should reject the propaganda (sometimes force) that tries to keep them out of the political arena, and should use, to the extent possible, the political opportunities that are formally available in relatively free societies like the US. They should also proceed well beyond this, aiming to dismantle the illegitimate power of private tyrannies – a rather recent development incidentally, hardly graven in stone. But that is a separate matter. What private power naturally fears is what an organized public should cherish: conversion of the political system into an instrument to serve the interests of the general population, not its tiny sectors of privilege and private power.

During the last ten days, you have visited six different cities of India. What are the main impressions that you retain from this visit?

I have strong and vivid impressions, but l frankly do not see why people in India should pay any attention to them. I'm willing to discuss them, but only on the understanding that these are superficial impressions, necessarily.

One day in the West Bengal countryside left me with quite positive impressions about village self-government. One could not mistake the eager and enthusiastic involvement of people in running their own affairs, the overcoming of caste, tribal and gender discrimination, the use of simple but critically important technology (women installing and maintaining pumps for drinking water), a women's dairy co-operative, etc. I'd like to learn more, but the little I saw was impressive in comparison to what I've seen elsewhere, or read about.

Most of my impressions, however, are from lecture halls and discussions. The lively intellectual atmosphere, cultural depth, and very high level of competence are apparent, and most exhilarating. On the other hand, it is painful to see heart-wrenching misery alongside great opulence, the notable persistence of feudalist attitudes, the extreme and wasteful inefficiency, the huge and destructive black economy that surely undermines economic development, and the pitiful waste of rich human and material resources. More narrowly, it is distressing to see outstanding scholars, some of the best in the world, unable even to obtain books and journals: apart from everything else, not a good portent for Indian society and culture. So, it's very much a mixed story; but I stress, these are superficial impressions.

This book need not end here...

At Open Book Publishers, we are changing the nature of the traditional academic book. The title you have just read will not be left on a library shelf, but will be accessed online by hundreds of readers each month across the globe. We make all our books free to read online so that students, researchers and members of the public who can't afford a printed edition can still have access to the same ideas as you.

Our digital publishing model also allows us to produce online supplementary material, including extra chapters, reviews, links and other digital resources. Find *Democracy and Power* on our website to access its online extras. Please check this page regularly for ongoing updates, and join the conversation by leaving your own comments:

http://www.openbookpublishers.com/isbn/9781783740925

If you enjoyed this book and feel that research like this should be available to all readers, regardless of their income, please think about donating to us. Our company is run entirely by academics, and our publishing decisions are based on intellectual merit and public value rather than on commercial viability. We do not operate for profit and all donations, as with all other revenue we generate, will be used to finance new Open Access publications.

For further information about what we do, to donate to OBP, to access additional digital material related to our titles, or to order our books, please visit our website: http://www.openbookpublishers.com

Knowledge is for sharing

OpenBook
Publishers